TWINNED WITH...

An adventure around the twin towns of Europe

TWINNED WITH...

*An adventure around the
twin towns of Europe*

ROB SELF-PIERSON

To Diana:

Because I remember you saying when I was 17 I'd one day be
good enough to write a book. I laughed and said if I did
I'd dedicate it to you. Thank you.

Here you go.

'A twinning is the coming together of two communities seeking, in this way, to take action with a European perspective and with the aim of facing their problems and developing between themselves closer and closer ties of friendship.'

Jean Bareth
A founder of the Council of European Municipalities
and Regions after the second world war

THE JOURNEY

THE JOURNEY

10

16

PORTUGAL

SPAIN

17

SWEDEN

DENMARK
33
34

UNITED
KINGDOM

42 HOLLAND

GERMANY

32

43 BELGIUM
44
45   1
     2
7
5
4   3
6
14
13
15

FRANCE

41
40
39   36
     37
38   28
29
27
30

31

26

CZECH REPUBLIC

25

AUSTRIA

9
8
12

24

SWITZERLAND

21

ITALY

35

23

18   19   20

22

THE
BEGINNING

I'm sitting on a sun lounger outside a gîte in the south of France. Two cows are lowing at each other in the distance, while four cats come up, one by one, and try to be my friend. It's happy, warm and sunny here. I feel very at home. You see, in the last couple of years I've become a *proper* European.

This feeling of Europeanness is the result of a 10,000-mile journey around the Continent. The sort of adventure that looks scarily impossible on paper but ends up being just about doable. The sort that introduces you to many new ways of living your life. The sort that attacks your relationship and slaps you across the face but repairs you to make you tougher.

Allow me to explain.

A few years ago, as part of another adventure (this time walking around the British Isles by full moon), I found myself limping past the welcome sign to my hometown Waltham Abbey. My journey had taken me everywhere, from Brighton to Whitby, Edinburgh to Grasmere, Falmouth to Greenwich. I'd got to know more about my country than ever before, and understand exactly what it meant to be British.

Throughout the year, I'd seen countless welcome signs to towns, and on each spotted the same two words. *Twinned with, twinned with, twinned with.* Wherever I went, it seemed the town I was visiting was 'twinned with' another – usually somewhere in France or Germany, but sometimes further afield, like in the Czech Republic or Austria. And I had no idea what that meant.

Passing Waltham Abbey's town sign that misty January morning, I could just about make out the following words:

Waltham Abbey. Last resting place of King Harold II. Charter market town. Twinned with Hoerstel, North Rhine Westphalia, Germany.

Before popping to the pub to say hello to a couple of old school friends I hadn't seen in ages, I decided to satisfy my curiosity and find out about this 'town twinning' thing. In a few minutes, I'd understand it all and could recover from my travels with a pint. Or so I thought.

Half an hour later, I was sitting in the Angel with Matt and Sam.

'So, what's it all about then, mate?' asked Matt. 'What did you find out?'

'The people in the tourist office had never heard of it,' I replied, flicking a nut onto the 70s carpet. 'And the town hall was closed.'

'That's shit, buddy,' said Matt, sipping his beer. 'Really shit. No-one knows nothing about stuff around here.'

'The old woman in the tourist office looked at me like I was bonkers,' I said. 'I've found contact details for someone called Norma instead, so I've emailed her. Apparently she's part of the Waltham Abbey Town Twinning Association. Or something. I'm sure she'll have the answer.'

Matt started to giggle into his beer. Sam and I, used to our friend's spontaneous laughter at his own thoughts, continued.

'Didn't they invite you to Holsten at school, Robbie?' asked Sam.

'It's pronounced *Hoss-tel*,' I said to Sam. 'I think. And no. Did they?'

'Yeah. For Credits Day. But you played snooker instead.'

'TWATS,' said Matt, beer now streaming from his nose. 'The Waltham Abbey Twinning Society. TWATS.'

Sam continued. 'Mr Finnan came round to our class and said you'd got the highest credits score so you could go for a visit. And you said no. Cos you wanted to play snooker.'

Memories of Mr Finnan's invitation trickled back. I remembered him telling me I'd won Credits Day so could visit a town with a special connection to our own. 'It's our *twin* town,' he'd said, before going on to tell me how wonderful it was and how I was lucky to have this opportunity. I won the snooker competition that year – and Mr Finnan never spoke to me again.

Ten years later, sitting in the pub, the boys and I reminisced about missed opportunities. The chance to play football for the county. Those times we could've stood up for ourselves in front of bullies instead of screaming and running away. And that weekend I could've visited my twin town.

'Wouldn't it be nice to have those chances again?' I said.

'Yeah – think what we could've said to Michael Agger instead of running away screaming,' said Matt, wiping the last of his beer from his nostril.

'I meant the opportunities to go to Europe when we were 15. Think what we could've done. Think of the stories.'

'Could've been bullied by Germans,' said Sam.

I looked down at the table.

'Don't be sad, mate,' said Matt. 'You can still go to Holsten.'

'It's pronounced *Amstel*,' corrected Sam.

'It's pronounced *Hoss-tel*, lads,' I snapped.

Matt, twiddling his wedding ring, put down his beer and looked at me, serious all of a sudden. 'Yeah, why not? Let's go to Holsten.'

'*Hoerstel*?' I queried.

'Whatever.'

'Why?' I asked.

'Cos you just said we should.' Matt smiled and hiccoughed.

'No, I just—'

'All right,' said Sam, sinking his pint. 'Next weekend. Let's all go to Amstel.'

Deals brokered and promises made on beer aren't worth the beermats they're dripped on. Furthermore, arranging trips with old friends in long-term relationships and marriages is the business of fools.

Both messages arrived at the same time the next morning. They chimed like death knells. Sorry, was the gist of it. Sorry, can't make it to Holsten/Amstel next weekend, got family/relationship stuff to do. Have a great time though. Tell us all about it when you get back. PS my head hurts.

Moments later, my phone rang. Unknown caller.

'Hello,' I said. 'Rob speaking.'

Norma was about half my height. This was mainly due to her curved spine, which meant she could only sit like I imagined a snail might. As we sat in the Waltham Abbey community centre, surrounded by white-haired folk armed with paintbrushes and easels, she rolled back a little to look me in the eyes.

'I've known your parents since before you were born, Robert,' she said, waving a paintbrush at me in magic figures-of-eight.

I smiled. 'Yes, so Mum told—'

'And your brothers. How are little Nicky and Davey?'

'In their mid-thirties—' I went to reply.

'And your dear father in his shoe shop. Colin. A wonderful man. And your mother, dear Marian. Yours is a family name nobody can forget, Robert.'

Norma wasn't a woman you could rush. She'd arrived an hour late for our twin town chat and spent the first twenty minutes reminiscing – and inviting other members of the watercolour group to look at me and tell me I was handsome.

When we got to town twinning, she had less to say.

'I'm going to put you in touch with the Varnskuehlers, Robert. They are wonderful people. They will look after you well when you visit.'

'Visit? But at the moment I'm just—'

'You will love Hoerstel, Robert. It is made up of four small towns. Each is as beautiful as the one before.'

'Isn't it Hoss-tel?' I asked Norma, shyly.

'No, never,' she snapped. 'I made the same mistake early on and got a serious ticking off from the Germans. H-O-E-R-S-T-E-L. In German, whenever you see two vowels together like that, you only pronounce the second. Her-stel.'

I smiled and sipped my watery tea. 'I've learnt something already. But how did the relationship begin, Norma? Why... *Hoerstel*?'

'Go and find out, Robert,' Norma suggested. 'Ask Bernhard and Elke.'

So I did.

* * *

'Elke? Bernhard?' I asked the tiny, square-haired lady and round, bearded man waiting at the airport.

They checked a photo in their hands, looked at my face, checked the photo again, and then, very politely, said: 'Robert? It is good to meet you. Welcome to Germany.'

I went to give Elke a kiss on the cheek. She offered her hand.

'Are you hungry?' asked Bernhard in a deep voice.

'I could definitely eat,' I said.

Bernhard and Elke looked at each other, confused.

'Yes. I am hungry. Food. Please. Lunch?'

'Great,' said Bernhard.

'We will take you for our favourite cake,' said Elke.

I'd only booked a long weekend in northern Germany. I'd planned to fly over, see the town, maybe chat to the mayor (if I had the balls), then head home with a couple of stories to share with the boys. Essentially, do everything I should have done ten years earlier.

'We have a lot for you to enjoy,' said Elke, as Bernhard drove us along winding streets and the wrong way around roundabouts. 'But you tell us if it is not correct for you or too much.'

'I'm sure it will be fine,' I said, slowing my speech and adopting a slight German accent. 'Whatever you show me will be great. Thank you.'

'You must stop that *now*,' barked Bernhard, braking heavily. 'You are being English. You are being polite and saying the opposite of what you mean.'

'Norma is not like that,' said Elke. 'She is like us. That makes us laugh.'

I laughed. They didn't.

'So, what my wife is saying is we have a morning of cycling around Bevergern for you. We are having friends over for dinner. We will visit the *Rathaus*—'

'Rat house?' I asked.

'How do you say? Our civic hall,' said Elke.

Cycling, dinner, this *Rathaus*. Nazi worship sites, visits to other town twinning members' houses, raw-pork lunches. You name it, the Varnskuehlers had lined it up.

'And the young people are going to take you out, too. So you can see what the youth people like to do in our town,' added Elke, smiling.

'That sounds terrible,' I said.

Elke and Bernhard laughed. 'Ha. You have a wicked sense of humour, Robert. We *do* like that.'

After cake-lunch, my hosts walked me across a grey square under grey skies. Elke pointed to a fingerpost with a big grin on her face. I looked up and read the sign:

Waltham-Abbey-Platz. Waltham Abbey, Grossbritannien
Partnerstadt von Hoerstel seit 1993

'We like you in our town,' said Bernhard. 'How are you feeling about this?'

'Ha. A *twinned with* sign,' I shouted a little loudly. 'I feel proud. Very happy and strangely proud, Bernhard.'

The next morning, following a freezing night in Bernhard's half-converted loft, I sat with Elke for breakast. Her husband had popped out to pick us up some bread. As I tried to take in as much ham as I could manage – so I didn't offend anyone – we got chatting about my trip.

'It is good that you visit us,' said Elke, brewing me a pot of tea. 'It is good that you have become part of town twinning, as you call it. You are young and we need youth.'

My eyes looked away. 'Um. I'm not really a proper member, Elke. More like a guest. A friend of Norma and guest of town twinning. I'm just quite curious.'

'Yes, Norma told me. But we like to think of you as a part of us. That is how it works,' said Elke, handing me a tea. 'We are friends. We are friends with Norma and then we are friends with Norma's friends. And she is friends with us and our friends. We visit each other and we share our homes. Milk?'

Town twinning, Elke told me, had started after the second world war. Following six years of blowing the crap out of one another (my words, not Elke's), Germany, England and France decided to rebuild. Not just structurally but socially as well.

'I'm sure my husband will tell you a lot more when you cycle.'

The sun was shining on the pretty little towns around Hoerstel as Bernhard – who, I was becoming convinced, had been created by Raymond Briggs – and I cruised around their lanes. The buildings were like none I'd seen before. This was my first trip to Germany and I was absorbing it all.

'The huge sloping roofs, Bernhard. Why are they so tall?'

Bernhard slowed to a stop beside a hedge outside a park. 'I think it is from the old farmhouse design, Rob. What is more interesting is what you find right here.' He pointed to the hedge.

'A hedge. Is it a... special hedge? A *German* hedge?'

'It is who could be buried here. A Nazi. Someone we should not name. An evil man might be buried in this park, and recently it has become a worship place for the new Nazis, the young Nazis who will never know the awful past.'

I breathed deep, my chest painful all of a sudden like I'd inhaled broken glass.

We cycled along an industrial canal and into Bevergern, where we visited the Anton Hilckman museum. Hilckman, Bernhard told me, was a German philosopher who was flung into a concentration camp during the war for his thoughts on the Nazi regime. He survived and went on to write hundreds of publications about politics, freedom, culture, identity and his hometown, Bevergern. There was now a street and guesthouse named after him.

'So Bevergern is a town like Hoerstel?' I asked Bernhard, as we reached his friend's house and left our bikes on the front lawn.

'It *is* Hoerstel,' Bernhard replied. 'Hoerstel is Bevergern and Riesenbeck and Dreierwalde and original Hoerstel. Together, we are big Hoerstel, your twin town. Or "*Partnerstadt*" as we say.'

'Ah yes, Norma told me. The four small towns that make up Hoerstel.'

'Rob,' said Bernhard, 'do you speak any of our German?'

Bernhard learnt the answer to his question the hard way, as he spent the next couple of hours translating for me and his friends – first the head of Hoerstel's town twinning association (their Norma) and later, in the *Rathaus*, the moustachioed *Burgermeister* (mayor). Both gentlemen shared information about their town with unbounded joy and boyish glee. I just sat and took it all in.

Waltham Abbey and Hoerstel twinned back in 1993. The people of Bernhard's town had decided they wanted a *Partnerstadt* and that it should be in England or France. So they put it to vote. The locals responded to the article in the local paper in favour of England – somewhere close to London, preferably. So the mayor and council got together and typed out an invitation to lots of little towns on the outskirts of England's capital.

Only Waltham Abbey responded.

Back in '93, my little Essex hometown sent a delegation to Hoerstel to meet the locals, have a few beers and get a feel for the town. Not long after, a small group of Germans visited Waltham Abbey. Although one visitor stormed out of dinner and caught an early flight home, most of the party enjoyed my town enough to give things a go. The two mayors signed a charter and everything became official. Waltham Abbey and Hoerstel were 'twins'.

That night, the Varnskuehlers invited their international friends over for raclette, a Swiss dish where your host brings out a giant electrical frying pan and you sort of cook your own dinner. Over wine, we chatted about Europe and how we should all work hard to keep it going. An idea started to brew in my mind.

The following day, Elke handed me over to the teenage children of another town twinning family with the promise that 'you will understand that the youth people of your twin have fun too'. Have fun and eat raw pork, I discovered at lunch, when we popped to a supermarket and ordered a lump of *Mett*. And snack on bratwursts and beer outside caravans at midnight. And drive really, really, really fast on motorways, like Hulk, a friend of a friend of a friend of the town twinning family.

By Sunday night, I was exhausted.

Bernhard dropped me back to the airport on the Monday morning, following my whirlwind weekend. As I went to join the tiny security queue, we shook hands and he asked if I'd had a good time in my *Partnerstadt*. 'Bernhard, thank you,' I said. 'It's been amazing. In fact, it's given me an idea.'

* * *

'Do it, buddy,' said Matt, sipping his beer.

'You did that moon adventure thing and became a proper Brit. Why not do another and become a proper European?' added Sam.

We were back in the dimly lit Angel in Waltham Abbey.

I put my notepad and a map of western Europe on the sticky table. 'Lads, you're right – I'm going to do it. I've set up a website to see if anyone else has a twin town they've never been to. Loads of people have emailed. So I've chosen quite a few towns to visit on a road trip. They're mostly in France and Germany. Though Prague's one as well. And I'll need to go to Denmark and Sweden and—'

'All in KT?' asked Matt.

'Yeah. Three months of driving. Why not?'

'No reason. I mean it'll be great. Really good,' said my friend.

'And expensive,' added Sam.

I hadn't done the full maths. The excitement of driving around the Continent to find out about Europe through the lens of town twinning was too exciting for that. What an opportunity. Just me, my new sports car and 45 strange new towns across 12 countries to explore and be delighted by. Like my Hoerstel trip, but with the chance to cruise between towns in a sexy motor. Everything was set up for my own little solo adventure. And then I met and started to fall in love with a girl called RG.

Instead of planning meticulously, my new girlfriend and I spent the few months before my odyssey drinking beer, visiting Cornwall, hanging out with friends and smooching on the streets of London. Rather than tracking down the Bernhards and Elkes of the towns I'd plotted on my beer-stained map, I glowed with sickly sweet new-relationship loveliness. Days disappeared in a haze of happiness. But departure date was looming and before I'd even reached my first twin town I felt sad to be leaving the UK.

'I'm going to miss you,' I told RG, one night at my flat.

'Why don't I come?' she asked.

'Why *don't* you come? I'd love you to come. It'll be lovely doing it together.'

And so RG went to work the next day and told her boss she'd been invited on a road trip around the Continent in search of twin towns and that she really wanted to do it. Her boss, to my surprise and delight, told her to go ahead – it would be great for her personal development and she'd come back buzzing, which was good for the company.

So I began to share everything I could with my new girlfriend. The spoilt map, the towns, the messages from the 45 people who'd got in touch, stories from Hoerstel, my new German words, the names of town twinners I'd run out of time to contact.

'So how's it going to work?' she asked, grinning.

'No idea,' I replied. 'Well, we're going to drive around Europe in my beautiful sports car KT and put the top down and have the wind in our hair and drink little

European beers and French wine and—'

RG stopped me. 'But the town twinning bit. I love the idea of meeting loads of fun people like Bernhard and his wife. How are we setting all that up?'

'Well that's the exciting thing,' I said, trying to hide the fact I'd been partying instead of planning for the last half a year. 'We're not setting anything up. We're going to do it on the hoof. Turn up, ask around, have adventures. All impromptu and fun. Excited?'

RG looked at me, as serious as I'd seen her. 'We should plan something, Rob.'

'We're going tomorrow, my dear,' I replied. 'Which reminds me, I didn't quite get around to ordering the European map thing for the satnav. Silly me.'

RG closed her eyes and shook her head. '*Bonne chance* to us.'

I smiled. 'That's the spirit... Wait, what does *Bonne chance* mean?'

What follows are 45 stories written as letters to the people who visited my website and asked me to go to their twin town. It's a good example of how to bumble around a continent for three months and absorb life as you go.

As a complete collection, this book is a tale of discovery, identity, duty, pride, confusion, love, bitterness, history, humanity, geography, of Europeanness and – at the heart of it all – a little thing called town twinning.

PART I

A FLYING
START

Hello Rob

My niece told me all about your little adventure (and that you're seeing each other – exciting!!). I've always wondered what on earth it means when a sign says 'twinned with'. You'll be satisfying the curiosity of lots and lots of people, I'm sure. Not least me.

I live in Harrow, which is twinned with the French town of Douai. Would you check it out for me please? I don't know anything about it.

Good luck and enjoy yourselves!

Shanta x

1 · Douai
Twinned with Harrow

—

In which important early lessons are learnt

Dear Shanta

As your niece and I drove from the ferry onto Calais soil – my first time motoring on the Continent – I shivered and let out a small shriek.

'You ok?' asked RG. 'Would you like a sweet?'

'Of course I'm ok,' I snapped back. 'I'm just concentrating.' Then I sneezed, wobbled, veered us in front of an articulated lorry and almost fainted. I think it's fair to say I felt a little nervous.

We reached your twin town, Douai, in the late afternoon. By this time I'd just about conquered my fear of driving on the right and was filled with terror at the adventure that lay ahead. It was mid-April and starting to get dark as we left our hotel and walked across Pont d'Esquerchin towards the centre of the town. Puddles and grey skies made us feel very at home.

'This is going to be great,' I said to RG, squeezing her squelchy hand. 'I can almost feel Norma here with me.'

RG looked at me. 'Who's Norma?'

Our coats dripped by the radiator inside Bistrot du Boucher, a suit-and-tie restaurant not far from Place d'Armes, the main square of the town. The waitress seemed ok with it – and with our scruffy trainers and jumpers.

Looking at the menu, RG and I discussed words that meant nothing to us, then requested those words in sounds that meant nothing to the waitress. But where the ordering process was a terrifying challenge, the anticipation of the food arriving was a joy. We decided we'd either ordered a plate of meat with mushrooms and other vegetables, or a pie. You can imagine our faces when a bowl of kidneys turned up.

'Shall we get some tap water?' asked RG. 'Y'know, celebrate the three months that lie ahead?'

'Of course, madame,' I replied, sipping my *vin de table* like a pro. 'Leave it to me.'

I cleared my throat.

'*Excusez-moi*, madame,' I said to the straight-faced waitress. '*Avez vous...*'

I blanked. No French came to mind. None. The twelve refresher lessons I'd signed up for back in London all of a sudden seemed a complete waste of time and money. All I could remember from those was '*Comment dit-on*', but I couldn't remember what it meant. So I started turning an invisible tap and making splashy water noises.

RG didn't look as impressed as I'd hoped. More disappointed. And parched. I dropped my head in embarrassment.

On the cold, wet walk back to the hotel, my girlfriend pointed to the sky. 'Looks beautiful,' she said, peering up to Douai's elegant bell tower. 'Be amazing to go up there. Maybe tomorrow?'

I shrugged a 'yes', still upset about my restaurant moment. 'We need to do some town twinning stuff, too.'

The next morning inside *l'office de tourisme*, a lovely young lady called Delphine told us people from Harrow liked to visit her little French town once a year or so to look around – and to get involved in something called the *Fêtes de Gayant*.

'But I am not good to speak to,' said Delphine. 'Madame Delecombre. She is good. From the town hall. She is part of the Committee of International Relations. I will invite her to meet with you. At this moment.'

Within half an hour, Marie Delecombre was talking us through Douai's six twinnings: Harrow, Seraing in Belgium, Recklinghausen in Germany, Pulawy in Poland, Kenosha near Chicago and Dédougou in Burkina Faso. This little lady, pink scarf laying neatly on her shoulders, had popped across town just to answer our questions.

'After the wars, France and Germany needed to do something to make relationships better,' she told us in perfect English. 'The relation with Recklinghausen started in 1965. Both towns chose to start it because the people wanted to do something. After the wars, we needed to create Europe.'

The idea of creating Europe fascinated me. As Marie continued to talk RG through Douai's relationships with its other twins, I imagined our continent without European identity. No EU, no common market, no (almost) single currency. No easy travel or trade. No penpals either side of the Channel. No neighbours pulling together to get through tough times. No quick trips to Elke and Bernhard. No Eurovision Song Contest.

'Each year, a group from your home comes to Douai. Always for the *Fetes de Gayant*,' said Marie.

'*C'est quoi?*' RG asked Marie, plucking a little French from somewhere.

We learnt how every year the Gayant family – Dad, Mum and the kids, Jacquot, Fillon and Binbin – walked the streets of Douai. The parade had been happening for centuries, but the giants changed from time to time. The latest version of these eight-metre *geants* had come to life after the wars. 'The Germans destroyed the ones existing before,' said Marie, looking sad.

'Ooh, can we get involved?' I asked.

'You are here at the wrong time of the year,' said Marie, shrugging.

I asked her about Douai's twinning with Harrow and learnt it was your town's closeness to London that had appealed to the people of Douai. Like Waltham Abbey's had to the people of Hoerstel. So the two twinned.

'Each one of our twinnings has a different story,' said Marie. 'Like Dédougou in Burkina Faso. Our people wanted to help the poor people there so we twinned. Twinning is beautiful for connecting people and sharing stories.'

Marie headed back to the town hall, wishing us *bonne chance* ('good luck', I'd learnt from RG) and telling us what we were doing was very important – for us and for European relations.

Just off the town square, we met a quiet man from the *beffroi* and followed him to the top of his tower. 'I have a little English,' Fabrice in his knitted jumper and glasses told us. 'It's probably better than our French,' said RG.

Fabrice and Marie, it struck me even this early in the trip, were examples of why town twinning worked. Sitting below the bells with Fabrice, banging the keys that rang them, I smiled to RG. Kind, friendly, thoughtful and considerate, Fabrice and Marie were clearly proud of what they did for Douai. They seemed proud of France and proud to be French, too. And they were happy to invite two curious Brits, neither of whom could even order tap water in a French restaurant, into their lives.

'Just by taking the time to pop into one another's countries – eat the food, drink the drink, try the language – we can keep these relationships going and make sure the Europe Marie's generation helped create isn't wasted,' I said to your niece, pacing around outside the town hall. 'I think we're going to have fun learning and exploring over the next few months, lady.'

RG squeezed my hand. 'Should be great, my dear. Should be *really* fun.'

As the evening started to set in and our time in Douai fade, we passed a war memorial. Beneath the statue of a man with fat shoulders and no neck pointing a crossbow at his foot, an engraving read:

1914-1918
la grande guerre

1939-1945
la seconde guerre mondiale

We stood in silence and thought back to our time inside the *beffroi*, when Fabrice had led us to the top of a stairway. On the walls we'd read the names of hundreds of former Douai residents, either killed, locked up or tortured during the wars. Each name, like each twin we planned to visit as part of the trip, had a unique story to tell.

That feeling of unity and what it meant to be European lingered as again the rain began to spit and the wind encouraged us south. We were about to head towards Albert, our second twin, and a place famous as the scene of one of the fiercest, bloodiest and costliest battles of the first world war.

Rob

Rob

This is my home town and twin town!
www.ulverstoncouncil.org.uk/town_twinning.php
I've never been. Please visit.

Sounds like you'll have fun!

Sara

2 · Albert
Twinned with Ulverston

—

In which there is a strange and touching coincidence

Dear Sara

We drove to Albert with heavy hearts – the idea of Europeans trying to wipe one another out was eating at me. As we crossed the Somme, there was no sound but the gentle hum of KT's engine.

On the 1st July 1916, 58,000 British men had died on these battlefields. It was the Allied push on the Western Front – an attempt to repel the German forces and cut their numbers. Although planned as a joint French-British attack, Sir Douglas Haig's men had to go it alone that summer's day, as the French headed south towards another German advance at Verdun.

Trench warfare, my shiny-headed history teacher would always drill into us at school, was muddy, mucky and absolutely unceremonious. He would often recite Wilfred Owen to reinforce his point. But it was only today – cruising stress-free through the heart of John McCrae's Flanders Fields – that those words would sink in, and this catastrophic failing of European togetherness would come to life.

The road to Albert was long, straight and timeless. A scar through the killing fields. Either side of it, memorials marked where men from across the world had fought and too often perished. At Pozières, Delville Wood, La Boiselle and other sites, simple stone markers demonstrated to me and RG how lethal Europe without unity could be.

'It's hard to get your head around it,' I said as we passed the towering Australian memorial at Pozières.

'I can't,' she said. 'Or I don't want to in some weird way.'

Tens of thousands of young men cut down by guns and bombs. Ripped to pieces by bullets, shrapnel and barbed wire – the latter used before the war to stop animals escaping farms in the United States.

'And now it's fields of beautiful flowers,' I said. 'And it smells like cabbage.'

Inside your twin town, the vegetable smells mixed with cigarette smoke.

'Wonder if a French market sounds like a market back home,' I said to RG, as we saw the last of the Albert marketeers shutting up shop for the day. *'Banane! Banane!'*

We smiled at the French men and women, who were smoking and chatting beside their stalls. RG then got out her phone and took a photo of a door.

You really do learn about someone when you travel together. Although we'd been dating for a while, I had no idea my girlfriend liked to photograph doors. While she captured an oaky moment at the top of some giant stone steps, I took in a nearby plaque. It read:

To commemorate the glorious heroes of the machine gun corps who fell in the Great War

1914 - 1918

175,000 men of all ranks served in the corps, of whom 13,791 were killed and 42,258 were wounded or missing. Upon the battlefields of which this place was a pivot were fought some of the most famous actions in which the machine gun corps distinguished itself.

To put these numbers into perspective, around 10,000 people were living in Albert at the time of our visit.

Sitting in our second restaurant of the trip, we performed better than the night before, now armed with 'carafe d'eau' for tap water. And we did ten times better than the white-haired English holidaymakers on the next table.

'Ham and cheese toastie,' said a large, round, loud lady. 'But no cheese. Without cheese. Minus the cheese.'

'Pardon?' asked the middle-aged waitress. 'Sans fromage?'

'No.' There was heavy tutting. 'No cheese. Nada cheese, por favor. DON'T. WANT. YOUR. CHEESE.'

The neat French lady frowned. I sensed she understood everything they said.

We ordered a croque monsieur and minced beef haché. 'À point?' asked the neat lady. 'Um. Oui, yes, please, s'il vous plait.'

It turned out à point meant medium-cooked. While raw was cru, rare was saignant and well done was bien cuit. Oh and blue was bleu. When the beef turned up, I realised the neat lady and I had a different idea of medium.

'Ok?' she asked, checking on us.

'Mmm,' I replied, wiping a little blood from my chin.

Outside, the weak spring sun fell between the trees and distant sparrows called to one another. Inside the restaurant, English people sat deep in English conversations ('that's a bit pricey for a ham and cheese toastie') and locals expressed themselves with dismissive shrugs and animated gestures.

After two days of driving, and now filled with a heavy meal, my mind wandered back to the Somme in 1916. The restaurant voices faded and all I could hear were whispers. Until an explosion almost burst my eardrums. Then came shouts and screams in conflicting languages. As I heard machine guns roar, I saw Matt and Sam falling to their knees ahead of me, their bodies assaulted by bullets.

Inside Musée Somme 1916, RG and I followed the story of the Battle of the Somme on the walls. The museum – around the corner from the stunning Basilica of Notre-Dame de Brebières, hit by a shell in January 1915 – throws visitors downstairs into trench life as they enter.

Pistols, rifles, bayonets, swords (used for opening mess tins and killing enemies) and grenades of all shapes and sizes, from bulb-shaped to giant-firework-rocket-shaped, filled the dimly lit cabinets. Plus a mess tin, a knife and fork, fingerless gloves for those harsh winter months and the occasional sketch of a naked woman.

We reached a door and pushed through, straight into the trenches.

'Hold my hand,' said RG, as the sounds of bombs and guns echoed along the corridor and the lights flickered.

Behind us, another British couple advanced. 'Hold my hand,' said the lady.

Back in the car, our energy levels fell and our eyes demanded rest. My back and mind were aching from the driving. I laughed at myself.

'The men and women who fought during the wars must've had tired eyes and aching minds *and* bloody blown-off limbs,' I said to RG. 'And I'm moaning about a couple of days of driving.'

'*And* they had to live in mud, wash in mud, sleep in mud and die in mud,' she added.

Although officially twinned in 1976, as a sign of friendship between the two towns, Ulverston and Albert had a deeper connection only discovered in 2006. Paula Flanagan-Kesteloot, a Brit who moved to France in 1992, spotted a trench called 'Ulverston' on a 1916 map of the Thiepval Wood and Ovillers trenches. Why was it there? Nobody seems quite sure. But it suggests there was a Rue d'Ulverston on the Somme almost a century before the characterless street named after your hometown in the clean and clinical housing estate we briefly walked around just outside of town.

Not far from Albert, we reached the most well-known memorial of the Somme.

'Mum and Dad said to come and see it,' I told RG, as we pulled up near Thiepval.

'Mum said when they popped over a couple of years ago she just wept and wept looking at the graves. Hundreds of gravestones, she said. All for fallen soldiers, most unknown.' Or 'Known unto God', as the memorial read. 'But then Mum is a bit mushy like that.'

This was our last stop before a drive south to the Paris suburbs and our next set of twin towns. It felt like duty – to pay our respects to the people who'd sacrificed their lives in order to give future generations like ours their freedom.

We studied the names inscribed in the memorial's stone walls, then turned to the gravestones, which sat in uniform lines: the French to the left, the Brits to the right. We read how Thiepval marked the bond of the French and British, who'd fought and died together numerous times between 1914 and 1918. A bond, it struck me, that was living on through twinnings like Douai and Harrow, and Albert and Ulverston.

Rob

Hi Rob,

Apparently, Burnley has been twinned with Vitry-sur-Seine since the 1960s. Who knew?

To give you a tiny bit of background about Burnley, it used to be a really industrial kind of mill town. Since all the mills disappeared, it doesn't seem like it's really had much of an identity – it's a bit of a tired old place, which is sad really.

BUT some lovely things are happening, apparently, and they're also to do with twinning. Like the twin town people who visited the homeless centre.

I hope this is a starting point and Vitry-sur-Seine makes it onto your list.

Let me know how you get on!

Kate

3 · Vitry-sur-Seine
Twinned with Burnley

—

In which things go a bit quiet

Dear Kate

We thought we'd been clever buying a European roadmap for the satnav the morning we set off. We also thought it was a smart move getting hold of a massive atlas of Europe as a backup. But we weren't smug for long.

The wifi we'd been stealing from cafés and hotels hadn't been good enough to install the map onto TomTom. And the massive atlas was so massive and zoomed out we couldn't spot the roads we needed. The Peripherique – Paris's answer to the North Circular – looked more like an elastic band than the terrifyingly giant labyrinth it was.

We reached Paris's orbital early evening. All we could see were grey, faceless commercial buildings and restless, bumper-to-bumper commuters racing home after a day's work. We hoped your twin town would offer us a world of quiet beauty hidden away from this industrial blahness. Maybe we should've known better, considering your description of Burnley as 'a bit of a tired old place'.

Eventually, we left the Peripherique and reached our hotel. There were three minutes until the check-in desk would close for the night. I parked up in a nearby Lidl car park as RG dashed inside and tried to make traffic small-talk with the moody proprietor.

'Everything ok?' I asked RG when she got back at the car.

'Miserable gitbag,' she replied. 'He wasn't nice at all.'

The next day, we took a break from twinning and enjoyed some time in Paris, the city of love. We walked along a bridge and waved at marathon runners. We took pictures of the gargoyles along the walls of the Notre Dame. We decided against paying ten euros for the Louvre and instead strolled through the colossal Jardin des Tuileries. And we accidentally got stuck in the middle of a massive Sarkozy rally, where France's president was fighting for re-election.

We walked along Champs-Élysées up to Arc de Triomphe then down Avenue D'Iena to the Eiffel Tower, where we laughed at tourists posing for photos. Then we took some ourselves. We ended up at a bar where young French people were chatting, smoking and discussing the rally. There, we drank a lot of Leffe and inhaled a lot of Gitanes. Paris, we decided, was a city puffed with pride. And its youth was very political indeed.

And then there was Vitry-sur-Seine. Foggy-headed and wheezy-chested the next morning, we headed into the Parisian suburb on foot.

RG had read somewhere that Vitry-sur-Seine was where the Paris hip-hop scene had begun. She was keen to find out more, but there were no signs of rap music. We'd found more hip-hop in Douai, where we'd seen boys cruising the streets with bass thumping through their hatchbacks. All we found in Vitry was a bit of half-hearted graffiti.

Centre ville (the centre of town) was made up largely of bus stops and gigantic blocks of flats. Not many people were walking the streets.

'So where are all the people who live in the big massive flats?' asked RG.

'No idea,' I replied, looking over my shoulder suspiciously.

Vitry-sur-Seine's *hotel de ville* was a modern red-brick building made of domes and archways with huge stained-glass windows. Although the walls cut out much of the natural light, the stained glass gave the foyer an otherworldly glow.

Inside, we found three uniformed ladies sitting behind a desk.

'*Bonjour. Parlez-vous Anglais?*' RG and I asked in romantic unison.

We'd learnt there was no such thing as a 'yes' or 'no' answer to this question. In fact, we didn't even mean it as a question. It was more a warning: *we're foreigners who want to have a go at your language but we'll very soon mess up. So please be nice.*

'*Joo-mer-large?*' I tried.

The smiley lady behind the desk shrugged.

Until this trip, '*jumelage*', the French term for town twinning, wasn't a word I knew. But we'd heard Delphine in Douai say it a few times and seen it written on a couple of town signs where 'Twinned with...' would have appeared in England. So we tried it.

'*Jumelage?*' RG repeated, a little less robotically than me.

Nothing.

'*Je suis researching pour a jumelage project,*' I said, mixing languages like a pro. 'Town twinning? Burnley?' (I may have even added a little Lancashire accent to 'Burnley'.)

'*Ah, oui, jumelage,*' said the nice lady, her '*jum*' so much softer than ours.

For the next ten minutes, Nice Lady at Desk led us along the corridors of Vitry-sur-Seine's town hall, popping her head through countless doors and asking people about *jumelage*. She got only '*nons*' and head-shakes in reply. We stood back, shrugging our shoulders, politely smiling and feeling thankful for the universal nature of body language.

Eventually, we accepted there was nobody around who could really help. Our guide took us back to reception to scribble down the address of someone in the committee who was on holiday till the following week. By which time we'd probably be in another country.

As she began to write, a tall, gaunt man appeared behind reception.

'Ah, this man speaks English. He speaks very good English,' said Nice Lady, again in very good English.

He was puzzled by our curiosity with his home.

'Vitry's a sleeping town,' he told us. 'This is where people come to sleep at night. During the day everyone goes to Paris to work and live. Vitry-sur-Seine is a town just for sleeping. See?' He pointed towards the three ladies at reception. 'Even they're asleep.'

He said there was nothing around. Nothing to see, nothing to do.

Walking towards the Church of St Germain, the shy sun bringing us some warmth, we came across some old paintings of the town. It looked charming – nothing like the place we'd walked through today. Perhaps it'd lost its identity the way you said Burnley has.

'Maybe we could just make it up,' I said. 'Tell Kate Vitry's like Eden, but a bit more French. It twinned with Burnley because of... gold.'

'Could do,' RG replied. 'I'm sure it'd come back to bite us though.'

Rob

Rob!

I spent a solid 18 years being dragged up in Hounslow.
It's twinned with Lahore and more recently with the Palestini-
an town of Ramallah, which caused all sorts of controversy.

Hounslow is pretty ethnically diverse and 41% of the
population was Asian at the time of the last census so
these twins do make sense – but Hounslow is also twinned
with Issy-les-Moulineaux in France. I don't think there are
many people in Hounslow that can tell you anything about
Issy-les-Moulineaux (I certainly can't) and I'd be really
interested to know if anyone there knows anything at
all about Hounslow!

Does it have a similarly jumbled population? Hmm well,
it's also got a Rennaisance style castle and The French
Playing Card Museum, and if that's not reason enough
to go, I don't know what is.

Bon voyage!

Chantal

4 · Issy-les-Moulineaux Twinned with Hounslow

—

In which Rob begins to lose heart

Dear Chantal

After a morning in Vitry-sur-Seine – a sleeping commuter town and concrete nothingness – our expectations had dropped. Nipping around the Peripheriques Sud and Nord like slightly hesitant locals, we'd started to spot countless Vitry-like areas. Tall buildings, billboards, layers of greyness and, on the surface, not much else. Issy-les-Moulineaux, we guessed, would be exactly the same.

Coming out of the Paris metro system at Mairie d'Issy, rucksack on my shoulders, I turned to RG. 'No-one looks at their mobiles on the Metro,' I said. 'They... talk to each other. Amazing.'

'Or read magazines,' said RG, who'd been reading a magazine since Pasteur, our connecting station on line 12.

Even in restaurants, it appeared the French liked to choose real conversation over texting, emailing, Googling, tweeting and Facebooking. Old and young. The twenty-somethings we'd studied in the café along Boulevard St Germain in Paris the day before seemed to enjoy chatting and smoking more than smart-phoning. And it was even more striking on public transport.

A burning smell from the train's rubber tyres disappeared as soon as we surfaced at Mairie d'Issy. The Gallic chatter from the Metro faded and a chill wind again welcomed us to a twin town.

About ten metres from the Metro exit, we found *l'office de tourisme*, where our new favourite French word again came in useful. *'Nous sommes recherche pour une projet de jumelage,'* I mumbled to the pretty girls in the office, using words I'd overheard in Vitry-sur-Seine's town hall. *'Issy-les-Moulineaux et Hounslow. Pourquoi?'*

I shoulder-shrugged and tried my 'intrigued' face. RG nudged me and said well done. We braced ourselves for a full and florid French response.

Instead, the two girls gave each other a look that said: *The words you speak are without doubt French words. But we're buggered if we know what the hell you're talking about.*

'Jumelage,' I repeated. *'Jumelage,'* a bit louder. *'Pour-quoi jum-e-lage?'* And in ten seconds I'd become DON'T WANT YOUR CHEESE woman from Albert.

The same happened in the centre administratif municipal. Another young girl at reception, but again someone who couldn't understand us. *'Jumelage,'* I repeated, until the penny dropped. The girl pointed us upstairs to the *troisiéme étage* (third floor) with the promise 'something is for you'.

Now, I'm a reserved man. The last thing I ever want to do is stick my head into a strange room, interrupt people in conversation and try speaking another language. But today, on the third floor of a municipal building in Issy-les-Moulineaux, just south of Paris, as part of an adventure I'd thrown myself and my new girlfriend into, there didn't seem any other option.

What French did I try? *'Excusez-moi. Parlez-vous Anglais?'*

And what came back? 'Yes. Of course.'

As much as trying to speak French was fun, it was draining. Every word took extra thought – both when speaking and listening. Menus were a minefield. Ordering tap water in a restaurant was a quagmire. So, after four days of fumbling for the right French phrase, this response came like news there was room at the inn.

A well-dressed rotund man with plenty of smiles, Sébastien invited us into his office and talked to us about Issy-les-Moulineaux and Hounslow.

At last count, about 65,000 people were living in Issy, he told us, sitting perfectly upright in his swivel chair. Nearly half of those were under 30. There were lots of schools and IT businesses. It was where the techies and media types lived and worked – the people employed by companies like Microsoft, Cisco Systems, Hewlett Packard and Canal + (France's premium TV channel).

But why twin with Hounslow?

'With 'ounslow?' said Sébastien. 'We have different types of relationship with different towns. For 'ounslow, it is more about schools. We do not have the money to do much more. It is Jane, our one person in 'ounslow. She manages everything there.'

In Issy, it was Sébastien who looked after it all, with the help of his three colleagues. As he bounced off to print us some factsheets, we flicked through a guide the girls in the tourist office had given us.

'*Le Musée de la Carte à Jouer et la galerie d'histoire de la ville*. We should go there,' said RG.

'*Carte à Jouer*? Is that playing cards? Why does that ring a bell?'

'There are 52 in a pack and you—'

'Oi. I mean the museum, yeah?' I said, giving RG a peck on the cheek.

'I know why,' she said. 'Because Chantal suggested we visit. It was one of the reasons she wanted us to come here. Though I think she meant that tongue-in-cheek.'

Thumbing through the guide, the Montquartiers caves looked interesting, too, with their million bottles of wine. And Les Arches, a collection of contemporary art beneath the city's aqueduct. And the wine path, and the botanical gardens *and* Le Ciné d'Issy.

Four towns in, we'd learnt something pretty big. Places where people live are full of stuff. Stuff needed for living – like houses, schools, hospitals and shops. And other, more interesting stuff – like parks, gardens and playing card museums. Even somewhere like Issy-les-Moulineaux ('a true Medialand', according to Sébastien's factsheet), which we'd guessed would be grey and dingy, had hidden treats. We'd also learnt that spending a day in each of these places wasn't long enough to really experience them. (Unless it's Vitry-sur-Seine. Then it's about a day too long.)

We picnicked in Parc Jean-Paul II, a short walk from the small church of St Etienne. 'Feels a bit like Stoke Newington,' said RG. 'It's got its own personality. Bit towny but still part of the city.' Holidaying kids swarmed around us while elderly couples enjoyed the sporadic spring sunshine.

From reading/poorly translating '*Guide pratique d'Issy-les-Moulineaux*' and speaking to Sébastien, it was clear Issy's relationship with Hounslow was ok but nothing great. Jane, some sort of magical, one-woman machine, was trying her best to get Hounslow involved in Issy life, but Sébastien had bigger fish to fry. Like Weiden in Germany, Macerata in Italy, Frameries in Belgium, and an unannounced Japanese twin.

'It is about inward investment more than culture these days,' Sébastien had told us. 'This is where the future is.'

Sébastien was the youngest person we'd spoken to who was involved in twinning. His ruddy cheeks had given him a boyish charm. But his talk of Far

Eastern relationships had made me question, for the first time, the purity of town twinning. Looking at the long list of twins on the town sign at the entrance to Issy at Port Versailles, cars rushing ahead of me, a tram about to run RG down, I wondered whether twinning was changing.

The idea that towns in France might twin for money instead of shared culture and values began to taint my view of the whole movement. Could my generation, I wondered, be responsible for turning town twinning into some sort of profit-making scheme? Or was it that already and I was just too naïve to realise?

Back in the centre of town, only one thing could lift my mood. The playing card museum. 'One of seven museums in the world dedicated to this theme,' said an excited RG, reading from yet another factsheet.

We skipped across the road and up to its big glass door. 'It's shut,' said RG, trying to force the door open. 'I want to cry.'

Rob

Rob,

All my experience (including going to France to celebrate the birthday of my penfriend of 35 years) came from my twinning with Jarrow and Epinay sur Seine, brought about by my penfriend's grandfather's left wing politics. He was the mayor and he wanted to be associated with Jarrow.

Epinay is now a rather downtrodden Paris '*banlieue*' and known for not much at all, but I spent some marvellous times there.

Happy to tell more if you're thinking of heading there to explore. Or maybe you can teach me something...

Sarah.

5 · Épinay-sur-Seine Twinned with Jarrow

—

In which the truth comes out

Dear Sarah

Issy-les-Moulineaux had left a bad taste in my mouth. Town twinning had started to feel a bit soulless and contrived. Swinging around the Peripherique Nord towards your twin felt like a visit to a distant relative you like the idea of visiting but deep down you're not sure you can be arsed to see.

In just a week, our adventure was feeling a little flat. We needed Épinay-sur-Seine to give us a spark, a story – something real, something human. We needed to meet a stylishly scruffy man called Gilles who could give up the secrets of his once thriving town.

My sports car KT had joined us on the Continent. I'd learnt from our time together back in the UK how she loved to cruise along motorways and through the Cornish countryside, where I'd been living when I bought her. I was learning she wasn't so keen on Peripheriques though. Or lumpy, bumpy, unfinished industrial roads. Or French one-way systems. On our second pass of Épinay, I managed to thump her over some sort of gulley and park up scarily close to a main road.

'We'll just pop in quickly,' I said to RG. 'Find the story then come back to KT. Quickly. *D'accord?*' I may have stroked KT goodbye.

Sundays to the French, it was becoming clear, meant a day off. So, we'd found, did Mondays. And sometimes Wednesdays. And the occasional Friday. Shops, tourist offices, town halls, museums – they were all closed some point during the week or weekend. But most of the time they were open. Unless it was lunch-time. Then the French liked to enjoy their lunch. Usually for a couple of hours.

Today was a Tuesday, so not an official unofficial day off. But it was lunch by the time we'd reached *l'hotel de ville*, which meant as hard as I tried to push the door it wouldn't budge. As we wandered around the streets, we found everyone was at lunch.

Inside Bistrot de Paris, I told RG about your email.

'Sarah's penfriend's granddad was mayor of this place. She said she had some great times here as a girl. But now it's a downtrodden *banlieue*. Can you believe they've been penfriends for 35 years?'

'What's a *banlieue?*' asked RG.

'It's a sort of... I don't know.'

As we looked out of the restaurant windows to Épinay, all we could see was grey. And rain. And a bit of grey rain. But it was fine – we were getting used to grey rain. It was the same grey rain that'd followed us from Dover and arrived with us in Calais. Wrapping up warm in our raincoats, we headed back towards the town hall.

It was an attractive sandstone building covered, like all official buildings in France, in political slogans. After accidentally getting stuck in the Sarkozy rally in central Paris, we'd begun to notice the political fervour around the capital. The presidential elections were about to kick off and lots of big French faces on campaign posters across Vitry-sur-Seine, Issy-les-Moulineaux and now Épinay were doing their best to sway the people of France.

Sarkozy was going with LA FRANCE FORTE, 'Strong France' or, as I liked to trans-late, 'Fortress France' ('As much as you want to, you'll never get in' *evil laugh*).

Francois Holland was keen for LE CHANGEMENT C'EST MAINTENANT – 'The change is now'. And Marine Le Pen, the far-right leader, liked a bit of LA VOIX DU PEUPLE, L'ESPRIT DE LA FRANCE, or, when the poster wasn't big enough for all that, OUI, LA FRANCE. Slightly worryingly – after what Bernhard had told me about the rise of the young Nazis back in Germany – it was Le Pen who kept popping up in the media.

My money was on a man who looked like the result of a face-on collision between Sarkozy and Geoffrey Rush – a chap called Jean-Luc Mélenchon. Mainly because of his funny face. But also because his slogan, PRENEZ LE POUVOIR, had a nice a balance to it (though it meant nothing to me, of course). As a bonus, his name made him sound like someone from Star Trek.

The revolving door at *l'hotel de ville* now revolved.

According to the lady behind the desk, who *really* couldn't speak English, we should head to the 'Culturel' at 3 Rue Mulot. She drew us a diagram to show it was a building a few doors down. We said *merci* and set off.

A muddy Seine gurgled to our left as we ambled through a quiet park. We walked between the trees, the rain thudding against our heads. After navigating a collection of community buildings and accidentally wandering through a school, we reached a man called Gilles.

Gilles was the perfect children's book Frenchman. While we spoke, he leant casually against a fireplace, his tight-fitting striped shirt rippling nonchalantly in the draught. His face was rough and his skin almond. In soft, sweet French-English he explained he wasn't the person we needed for the story of Épinay's twinning with Jarrow. 'But you ask me about film and I tell.'

In 1907, we learnt, the industrialists Charles Jourjon and Ambroise-Francois Parnaland established Éclair, France's third film production company after Gaumont and Pathé, in Épinay-sur-Seine. Éclair employed some of the most famous French film stars of the time. In 1911, the production company hit it big, opening studios in the United States. By 1912, when 'the Father of the Animated Cartoon' Emile Cohl joined, all was rosy.

Dorothy Gibson, fiancée of Éclair's president, brought the production company yet more success. She was a passenger on the Titanic. With the story of its sinking fresh in her mind, she spoke to her husband-to-be about turning her experience into a movie. In May 1912, just a month after the most famous maiden voyage in history, Éclair released 'Saved from the Titanic', with Dorothy Gibson playing herself.

Sadly, the studios went up in flames in 1914, taking this first film adaptation of the disaster with it. And a lot of the world's earliest film.

'It was tragic,' said Gilles, drawing smoke from his cigarette like a movie star.

One hundred years on from Éclair and Épinay reaching their peak, your twin town seemed more like a forgotten friend of Paris than place for pioneers.

'It's not good today,' said Gilles, his creased face now downturned.

'But things are changing?' I asked, pointing outside to the cranes, diggers, hoardings, builders and unfinished roads.

'Yes. It's change. All of this, it's change. It grows here. More businesses come so the *banlieue* must grow. Sorry, the... *suburb*.' He shrugged and smoked.

According to the plaque beside the studio gates, '*Si les années 1960 marquent la fin d'un âge d'or, la longevite des Studios Éclair demontre son adaptation aux evolution de l´índustrie cinematographique*' – though the golden age of French film is over, Éclair showed it could adapt. I wondered if the European continent my girlfriend and I were experiencing had also passed its golden age. And whether *it* could adapt. From the good and the bad we'd learnt about town twinning so far, it was too early to say.

The golden age for Épinay might also have ended, but your twin wasn't without charm. The world's biggest salad and haché in Bistrot de Paris had brought big smiles to our faces. And the walk along the Seine, although wet and sloppy, was beautiful. But it was obvious Épinay was a changing place: a *banlieue* with a fascinating and important history, but no real sense of identity as it prepared for the future.

Gilles, our chipped and scuffed friend from the cultural department on Rue Mulot, had brought it to life for us. He'd given your twin its personality. And for the first time we realised not meeting the head of the twinning association or international relations chief or mayor didn't mean failure. In fact, perhaps the real treats of a town and secrets to the success of town twinning were hidden in the locals.

Rob

Rob

My home town is Marlow, Bucks, which is twinned with
Marly-le-Roi in France. That's pretty much all I know apart
from that they should have exactly the same bridge. Good
luck with this, it's a great idea!

Isley

6 · Marly-le-Roi
Twinned with Marlow

—

In which there is the most beautiful spot in the world

Dear Isley

Just before we'd reached France, we realised something quite important about one of our twins.

A few towns in France share their name with districts of Paris, I'd learnt from my sticky, knackered map of western Europe. That meant there wasn't just a Cormeilles in the capital – another *banlieue* of the city – but there was one up near Rennes, too, in Normandy. And another a bit north of there. And another not far again.

It was the one near Rennes we needed for this trip. It was twinned with Chepstow, someone called Sue had told me over email. But when we plotted it on our map before setting off, we'd mistaken it for Cormeilles-en-Parisis. Bugger. This meant instead of enjoying a full day in Marly-le-Roi, we had to swing by on our way to Normandy.

Following our chat with Gilles just north of Paris, we'd decided we needed to meet more locals to bring twinning to life. We needed to get better at seeing things and doing things, as well as meeting twinning experts like Marie and Sébastien. And we needed to explore more.

After a stopover in Louveciennes, a ruler-straight street of hotels and restaurants along the Seine (offering the full American dining experience), we reached your twin. We felt tired and hungry. But the signs were good. For the first time since Douai, we found a town centre with *boucheries* and *patisseries* and *charcuteries.* And from a nearby streetmap, we guessed we could walk the whole place in a few hours, giving us plenty of time to get to Cormeilles.

'Have you noticed something?' asked RG.

'It's nice,' I responded. 'And there's a butchers and cake shops and a meaty place.'

'Yes. There's all that. And everyone has a baguette under their arm,' she said, pointing at the locals. 'Loads of baguettes but no bakery. Weird or what? I really want an authentic baguette now.'

Half an hour later, back where we started, we were still without Frenchstick.

'There has to be a bloody *boulangerie*,' I said to RG, stomping like a child. 'It's a French town, so it's like the law. And everyone's carrying bloody bread.'

RG remained silent.

'It'll be down here,' I said, looking along a cobbled street.

Ahead, another couple checked the shop windows – also for signs of baguette, I guessed. 'Or maybe there's one here,' I said, pointing along another random road.

But RG had gone. Not yet in body but, from her lack of bounce, definitely in spirit. For the last few days, we'd been eating ok and sleeping pretty well. But our energy was coming from adrenaline, from enthusiasm, from anxiety, from the challenge of reaching 45 twins in 12 countries in just three months. And it was coming from spirit. For the first time in almost a week, we'd lost our oomph.

'Excusez-moi, monsieur. Baguette? Boulangerie? Dans la ville? Ici? Ou?' I asked yet another baguette-zombie.

The man who'd just slid out of a beaten-up Citroën fed me some directions.

On our way to Gennevilliers, the *banlieue* we'd ended up staying in when visiting Épinay-sur-Seine, I'd asked a little old dog-walking lady for directions. She'd responded with a couple of *droites* and *gauches*. Thankfully, as soon as we pulled out of the cul-de-sac, we spotted out hotel on the next corner.

Hunting down a spirit-lifting baguette would be a far bigger challenge.

Descendre. Gare. Escalier. Troisième. All words I recognised from my French refresher lessons. But, when the man from the Citroën stuck them together while flailing his arms, they lost all meaning. Confusion stopped me concentrating, which stopped me listening. I just stared at him and forgot everything.

'What did he say?' asked RG, when I'd caught up with her.

'The good news is there's a *boulangerie*.'

Her big brown eyes got bigger and her lips formed a sweet smile. 'That's great news, my dear. Where is it?'

'Well, here's the thing...'

Our friend definitely hadn't mentioned a giant park. So why we were now walking through its gates, past a bust of Thomas Jefferson ('*symbole de l'amitié Franco-Américaine*'), I couldn't say. But we plodded on.

According to signs inside, Le Parc Royal was once the playground of King Louis XIV. In the late 17th century, the king got tired of the ceremony of Versailles so commissioned a new royal residence in the forest of Marly. There he planned to spend time entertaining his favourite people.

The King went for a series of pavilions in a landscaped garden, designed by his chief architect Jules Hardouin-Mansart. The estate consisted of great ponds, a large water place for his horses, paved walkways, an entrance lodge, a chapel, and – at its heart – a chateau. But, in a big error of judgement, no bakery.

At the time, those who visited knew Marly as 'the most beautiful spot in the world'. Standing on the foundations of a maze, facing down towards *le grand bassin*, we tried to spot the chateau. From nearby information boards, it looked spectacular – a two-storey, modestly-sized building with tall windows, what appeared to be a roof terrace and just enough gold decoration to show it was a king's. Unmissable.

We looked back to the pine trees lining the path we'd walked along to reach the maze, and across to other pine-tree'd paths, and we checked the boards again, and looked up the hill, then east and west, and we jumped across the maze stones, and the rain started to fall in great sheets across the park, and still we saw no sign of the chateau.

So I did the only thing I could think to do. I tried to start a conversation on Twitter, so I didn't have to tell RG that yet again I had no answer.

The message said:

'What a lovely little place. Marly le roi. A getaway for Louis XIV. We're in his gardens now. But no sign of le roi...'

Within seconds, our good friend Harry had replied from London:

'As-tu déja vu le Chateau?'

After a little more tweeting with our friend, I worked out we weren't standing on Louis XIV's favourite garden maze after all. These were the foundations of his chateau. It was demolished in the early 19th century for its materials. The estate was partly restored in 1930 and had become part of the Public Establishment of the Museum and National Estate of Versailles.

'Just heard from Harry,' I shouted to a drenched RG.

She smiled. 'Really?'

'Yeah. Turns out the chateau is actually the maze, which isn't a maze, it's the remains of the chateau.'

'We're idiots,' said RG. 'The board said something about *démolis*.'

'Yeah, you're an idiot,' I replied, tweaking her waist.

After a long wander around the grounds of the King's estate, now a place for locals to walk their dogs, we'd bonded over our joint uselessness. But it was chatting with Harry over Twitter that'd really given us the push. It'd felt nice to know there were friends out there to help us during tough times that might lay ahead.

Inside the tourist office just outside the park, a frumpy lady told us that 2012 was the 40th anniversary of the twinning between Marly-le-Roi and Marlow. And inside '*Vivre à Marly*', a little booklet we picked up, there was a whole page dedicated to *les jumelages*. At the top there was a photo of The Compleat Angler on the Thames – perhaps close to the bridge you mentioned. Sadly we didn't find its twin structure in Marly.

'Bet they do a super-delicious Sunday roast in there,' said RG, looking at the pub.

'Or baguette,' I replied.

The road to Marly's station was long and curved, like a delicious croissant. We walked it wrapped in many layers, like a delicious club sandwich. Contact with a friend from home had lifted us. But food would top off a lovely few hours visiting your twin.

'*Boulangerie?*' we tried a couple more times, but nobody – not even the people carrying the baguettes – seemed to know where to find it.

Then, like a mirage, the Chez Jules bakery appeared by the station.

'Shall we?' I asked my travelling companion.

'Let us.' RG beamed.

Rob

Hi Rob

My late father in law started the twinning between
Chepstow in Gwent and Cormeilles in Normandy. That
was back in 1972 and he was vicar of Chepstow at the time.
Chepstow Castle was built by William Fitz-Osbern, Knight
of Cormeilles in the 11th Century.

People visit every summer on an alternate basis. In my
father in law's day the people of Chepstow would put on
a hog roast in the castle grounds. I hadn't realised but it
seems twin towns are dying off. Is that right?

All the best

Sue

7 · Cormeilles
Twinned with Chepstow

—

In which KT gets into trouble

Dear Sue

RG had researched and fallen for a charming little B&B in Cormeilles just before we left Marly-le-Roi. It was called Le Relais Normande. According to its website, it was run by a sweet-looking couple called Michel and Chantal. Sadly, we couldn't book it online and they wouldn't answer their phone.

'I'll park here and we can walk up the high street to find somewhere to stay,' RG said to me, a little crestfallen that Le Relais might not happen. We stepped out of the car, a bit shaky after RG's first drive abroad. 'What's that smell? Smells like booze. And fruit.'

'Look,' I said, 'that place says "*chambres*" in the window. Why don't we just stay there?'

RG looked up and noticed we'd parked three feet from Michel and Chantal's place.

We tapped on the window. Nothing. Banged on the door. Zilch. So I decided to trespass down the alleyway and look for another way in.

After ten minutes, I emerged to find RG calling my name up the other end of the street.

'Said the whole thing in French,' I beamed. 'The old chap told me he has a room. I saw it and it's lovely. Think he wants us to take our bags up now. Or eat a potato.'

With big chains, pinky rings and a smoking cigar, Michel wouldn't have looked out of place in a Guy Ritchie movie. But in his chef's get-up, with his warm smile and while holding a plate of 16 glistening crème brulées, his look was more Aled than Vinny Jones.

Upstairs in our wonky room, RG and I plotted how to meet more locals, make some friends like Bernhard and Elke in Hoerstel, and become better 'town twinners'. So far we'd met quite a few people. But they'd all been council types and we'd only spoken about technical twinning – the history, the meaning, the reasons. We had a feeling the joy of town twinning was in getting to know the locals. Or at least doing the things only they knew to do.

The laughter downstairs suggested our hosts already had the knack of this socialising business.

'Can you hear that?' RG said to me, as I was standing on the wonky floor and staring out of the sash window to KT, who was sandwiched between a couple of dented Renaults.

'Is it the sound of two beaten-up old heaps getting too close to KT?' I asked.

'It's the sound of people having fun, Rob,' she replied. 'Remember that?'

The next morning, we sat alone for Michel's bakery breakfast. Soon, a grey-haired man with surly disposition came in. He sat in a corner and read his paper. He mostly kept to himself, but indulged in a little gossip with Chantal, Michel's wife. A well-made-up lady with a big coat and good hair joined him twenty minutes later. After playing with Le Relais's perfectly coiffured terrier Valentine, the old gentleman spent some time lampooning the lady. Michel and Chantal took it in turns to join in. Half an hour later, kisses passed between lips and cheeks as the man and lady parted to start their days. I imagined this was the group's daily ritual.

We finished breakfast and popped to *l'office de tourisme* to perform our own ritual – trying to find out from a youthful, pony-tailed French guy what the locals did. He pointed us towards a steep hill and said, 'You walk and enjoy. But the weather...' He paused, clicking on his computer mouse to check the forecast. 'You have coats?'

We pulled on our Parkers in Pockets and trotted towards the hill.

Within about two hundred yards, RG and I were arguing. And thick black clouds were moving in. RG felt we needed to go straight a little longer, following the blue lines painted on the trees. Something about 'that's what the man said'. But to me it was clear we needed to take the first right and follow the blue cross. I could feel it.

Ten minutes later, we started the walk again – waving as we passed the pony-tailed man in the tourist office. 'Maybe it's a storm I'm feeling,' I said.

Out of town, we found nothing but fields, gravel tracks, trees and open skies. The low-hanging clouds were darkening and creeping closer. We stood and watched as streaks of violet rain fell like archers' arrows on the town. Breathtaking. But potentially drenching. So we picked up the pace.

As we passed a mob of curious cows, we watched as a lightning bolt flooded the sky and thunderclap shook the trees. The cows wobbled and the rain we'd admired in the distance arrived at our faces. We dashed back down the hill into town and up the steps to our room in Le Relais. Outside, boulder-like hailstones fell from an angry sky.

I ran straight to the window. 'You should see this woman trying to park behind KT.' I smiled. 'You could get a tank in there. She's rubbish. Back, forwards, back, forwards. Million point turn. Wonder if they teach that—'

'What's wrong?' RG asked me.

'She just crashed into KT.'

Walking past the twin town sign at the edge of Cormeilles – RG having dragged me away from my slightly chipped sports car – we worked out the boozy, fruity whiff. It was the Busnel distillery, where we were about to learn how locals captured the spirit of the region and bottled it as Calvados.

A charming English-speaking lady at the front desk told us we'd missed the last English tour of the distillery. But, she said, we were just in time for the last French one. She let us tag along for free, wishing us – a little ominously – good luck.

Our French skills had improved since the restaurant drama in Douai. But the language of the distillery tour was still too technical. A short, old, spiky-moustached and bigoted Frenchman called Jean-Pierre hung back from his group to explain what was going on. To add richness to his translations, he littered his stories with some casual racism about Chinese and Pakistani people.

A sweet-smelling dampness hung around the distillery's barns. RG said it reminded her of family Christmases. 'That spicy, cinnamon-kissed cider warming my insides before it's even reached my mouth. Yum,' she said.

As we prepared to leave, the tour group gathered. Many elderly people eyed one another suspiciously, like the town's cows.

'You don't go now,' said Jean-Pierre. 'This is only the beginning.'

A purple-haired lady's earlier eagerness to finish the tour now made sense. She wasn't there for the talking. She was there for the tasting.

Just outside reception, we sampled the Busnel Pommeau de Normandie. A split-second sharpness gave way to a refreshing sweetness, which gave way to a warming sensation in my chest. RG gulped down the lot to the shock of the others.

I tasted a creamy blend and said to the experts around me, 'It's a bit like Baileys.'

'Yes, but better,' was the purple-haired lady's snooty response. Then, with a smile, '*Je suis Normande!*'

(RG managed a glass of that too.)

'Who is drive?' asked a man in a raincoat that doubled his girth.

We both shook our heads. 'We are staying in Cormeilles tonight.'

Back in Le Relais, with more chatter downstairs, I took up my usual position by the sash window. RG checked the Chepstow twinning website and read how they'd kept the relationship going since your father-in-law started it back in 1972. She smiled as she told me about the people of Chepstow putting on a hog roast for their French visitors.

'Did you know Chepstow Castle was built by William Fitz-Osbern, Knight of Cormeilles, in the 11th Century?' RG asked me, reading from your email.

'Fascinating,' I replied, not looking back at her. 'Did you know French people can't park for toffee?'

Rob

Hi Rob,

I am intrigued by your project.

I work in Truro – the fourth smallest city in the UK –
which is twinned with Morlaix in Brittany. I have visited
Brittany several times, but I have never been to Morlaix.

What intrigues me about this twinning is that, rather than
having a social, political or even military link as other twinnings appear to have, the two locations apparently look very
similar – both have cathedrals, both have large viaducts,
both are positioned on rivers, close to the sea.

I once saw a logo that had been produced by the local
twinning society – it depicted Morlaix, but looked like
Truro. And then there is the 'celtic' connection – in
language, in food, in games and in stripy Breton tops.

So what does it feel like to be in Morlaix? How strong is
the deja vu? Will you see people or places that you know?
If you phoned back to Truro, would you be there too?

Truro has named its bypass after Morlaix.

Neil

8 · Morlaix
Twinned with Truro

—

In which something happens to RG

Dear Neil

A funny feeling crept into my stomach as we crossed from Normandy to Brittany. I hoped it wasn't the intestines I'd eaten in Cormeilles.

'Rod?' I asked, lowering KT's window to warm sunshine.

The man on the steps of the gallery in Huelgoat smiled. 'Yep. Rob?'

'Sorry we're late. Just getting the hang of this driving on the Continent thing,' I said. 'Not easy to find a place like Hoo-el-goat without a satnav.'

'It's pronounced "Whell-gwa",' said Rod.

Rod was husband of Mel, a Cornish artist I'd met through Twitter. They'd recently moved to Brittany and begun to convert a farmhouse. In a brief conversation we'd had before setting off, Mel revealed her family had a flat in Huelgoat (never pronounced 'Hoo-el-goat'), a pretty little village in the heart of the region. It sounded perfect for the Brittany leg of our tour, where five twins were waiting for us.

'Here are the keys,' said Rod, rubbing his thin ginger beard. 'I've put the fire on for you. There's some milk in the fridge, bit of cereal, croissants – though you'll get better and fresher in the bakery just across the road.'

Rod showed us upstairs. Big living room with crackling fire and Mel's seascapes decorating the walls. Big, wooden-floored, open kitchen with dining table and hob. Big bedroom. And shower. And bath. Both big.

These things might sound like nothing. A bit of space, a settee, natural light, pretty things on walls. But to a couple of road trippers who for a week had been staying in €40 hotels in Lidl's backyard, every appliance brought new joy. Electric heater. Wow. Toaster. Marvellous. *Kettle?* I almost wept.

RG and I hugged and kissed, like we'd just bought our first home.

After a cuppa and invitation from Rod to have lunch with him and his family in a couple of days, we sat down on the big settee and planned our trip to your twin.

'I feel a bit funny,' I said to RG, relaxing by the dancing fire.

'Is it the intestines you ate in Cormeilles?' she asked.

'No, it's Brittany. Those roads we drove down to get here, the tracks, they felt so familiar. Talk about déjà vu. It's just like Neil said.'

The next morning it happened again. Flying along the D769 from Huelgoat to Morlaix, I could've sworn I'd driven the road before. When we weren't lined either side by thick forest, it was villages with tiny churches, single-pump petrol stations and curious locals. The road meandered, going up and down slight gradients – perfect for a little straight-lining in KT. In the villages, locals strolled across the road in front of cars or pulled up in the middle of the road to chat to neighbours, and nobody raised their voice or beeped their horn. It all felt so familiar.

We parked up the hill from Morlaix's quayside.

'I've worked out the funny feeling,' I said to RG.

'It was the oniony intestine dinner thing you had with Michel and Chantal, wasn't it? I tried to tell you but you never listen,' she said.

'No, silly, well maybe a bit, but it's more because Brittany is Cornwall.'

'Hm. Maybe that's why we've got all these Cornish twins in Brittany,' said RG. 'Morlaix and Truro, Douarnenez and Falmouth, Benodet and Torpoint.'

'Yes. YES. Must be. Guess we'll find out.' I looked out to the harbour. 'This isn't Truro's twin. This *is* Truro.'

In 2011, while living in Falmouth, I'd put an exhibition together for the Cornwall Design Season at Truro's Lemon Quay. Truro, for a month, became a second home. (If you look up at the phone line outside Rowe's bakery, you might still see the extension lead I couldn't recover.) Here, in Truro's twin, there was something very Cornish in the air.

Rod had left a book about Brittany in the Huelgoat flat. Sitting on a bench in front of the quay in Morlaix, eating leftovers from the night before and looking out to bobbing yachts with tinkling bells, I delved in.

'Did you know in the 4th century people from the South West jumped on ships to avoid the Saxons, who were spreading across their country?' I asked RG. 'Some were happy to stay and give the invaders a chance. They probably thought the Saxons would bring over some cool stuff like the Romans had. But the Saxons were a disorderly bunch, it seems. So people who didn't like the idea of slipping back into bad habits headed to France.'

The bells on the boats continued to sing in natural arrangement as I read on.

'They ended up in Armorica, where the Romans were still living. The Brits, mainly Celts who'd been in Britain for at least a thousand years, settled here and set up a mini version of the Britain they'd just left. It was a "little Britain" or "Brittany".'

'And that's the end of today's lesson,' said RG, taking a gulp of vegetable pasta.

'Oi. Cheek. Less of that or it's detention for you.'

It was a Saturday, our second since starting the adventure. That meant everything was shut. There was no-one to talk to and no-one to learn from.

My phone beeped. It was Rod.

'Right, we've got a date with a man called Tim,' I said to RG, as we climbed some steps towards the town's viaduct. 'Apparently he can tell us all we need to know about twinning between Cornwall and Brittany.'

'Great,' said RG, looking sad. 'Go enjoy that. But will you drop me back?'

'Yeah, once we've met Tim,' I replied.

'No. Now. Please. I want to go home.'

'Home?' I asked, my heart stopping. 'You want to go *home?*'

'Back. I meant *back*. I want to go back to Huelgoat. I need a bit of time alone.'

My girlfriend's humour had dropped and her desire to learn more about town twinning was being outweighed by her desire to sit down and drink tea by a fire. I took it as a sign of tiredness. After all, we had just climbed a billion steps. In a moment, she'd become more zombie than travel companion.

Within an hour, RG was having a cuppa with Rod back at Mel's flat while I was driving towards an Englishman called Tim.

'Tim?'

'Bonjour,' said the voice on the other end of the phone. 'Oui.'

'Tim. Rob, Rod's friend,' I said. 'I'm on my way to yours but I'm lost.'

'Hi Rob. What can you see?' said the friendly voice.

I told Tim I could see a graveyard in a town called Berrien. He told me that was bad because I should be seeing a graveyard in a town called La Feuille. I told Tim I was nearly out of petrol. He told me that was bad because the nearest petrol station was back in Huelgoat.

It was decision time. Head back to Huelgoat, hope to find the petrol station, fill up, try to find Tim again and risk being an hour late for our meeting. Or hunt for La Feuille and hope not to get involved in any tiny-country-road situations that would lead to KT's tank running dry.

As Mother Nature blew a heavy cloud over my head, I eased my foot onto KT's accelerator and followed the road as it became narrower and narrower. It was just the two of us now.

Rob

Hi Rob,

I love the sound of your adventure and thought I'd contact
the town of Great Torrington where I live in Devon to see
if I can gain any information about Roscoff, the town it's
twinned with, in Brittany.

I have to admit, I can't recall learning anything about Roscoff
while at school! So it would be awesome if you were able to
visit and find out more so awareness could be raised.

Great Torrington has tons of history (civil war etc) so I
imagine Roscoff could be the same and twinned for that
reason. Or for its driving habits.

Kim

9 · Roscoff
Twinned with Great Torrington
—

In which an artichoke leads to an onion

Dear Kim

Rain started to fall and village centres merge into remote farms as KT's petrol indicator wobbled around empty. *One last corner*, I thought to myself, *and if I don't spot the sign Tim said to look out for I'll turn back*.

I took a deep breath of country air and drifted around the hedge. And there, hanging from a tree, was the artichoke logo swinging in the breeze.

'Hi Rob,' said a tall, bearded man in a cheque shirt waiting for me in the gravel. 'You found us then?'

I'd never felt so pleased to see someone I didn't know.

Rod's friend Tim made me a cup of tea and offered me a homemade yumyum before giving me a tour of his ceramics and textiles studio.

'Rod tells me you're finding out about Huelgoat and St Just,' he said, leading me back to his kitchen.

'Sort of,' I said, sipping my cuppa. 'I'm finding out about town twinning – the whole phenomenon. Not Huelgoat specifically, but towns all across Europe. Friends and strangers have told me where to visit, and I'm driving around with my girlfriend trying to find out what it's all about. This morning it was Morlaix. Tomorrow it's Roscoff.'

'Onions,' came a woman's voice from the next room. 'Roscoff. Onions.'

I looked to Tim.

'Amanda,' he explained. 'My wife. Must be cooking onions. Anyway, I'm part of the Huelgoat twinning association,' he went on. 'But I don't know about Morlaix or Roscoff. Just that Morlaix and Truro feel very similar, right?'

'Hugely,' I replied. 'Rod said you might be able to shed a little light on the whole Cornwall-Brittany thing.'

Tim's wife popped in from next door. 'Hiya, Rob. Tim – tell him about when the French took you down to the cellar. Ooh and the coach trip. That says a lot about the Bretons and the Cornish.'

Amanda gave me a grin.

'Yeah, tell me about that, Tim.'

* * *

The next morning, RG and I followed signs to Roscoff. To avoid further driving dramas, KT now had a full tank of petrol. While I had Tim's stories swimming around my head and RG, after an afternoon of chatting with Rod and relaxing by the fire, had new energy. Her eyes were alive as she drove us along more winding tree-lined lanes.

Chilly spring sunshine welcomed us to your twin. We saw blue skies and palm trees and rundown Renaults and tanned, leathery faces and shiny yachts and, as we stepped from the car, we heard London voices.

'See that?' one tanned Brit asked another, pointing to a huge boat. 'That's got three uncle chains connected to the duckbill, and under the chassis there's a hydrolimpet that doubles up as a barnacle buster.' Both men nodded and petted the vessel lovingly.

Near the harbour, locals and holidaymakers were queuing at a *frites* shop to get a box of fries. RG and I, loaded with more homemade leftovers, walked on, hunting for signs of Roscoff's relationship with your town. Under a leafy archway, we stopped for lunch as furious clouds floated in on a chilly wind and stole our sunshine. My girlfriend tutted as another downpour soaked our feet.

'Want to hear a story to cheer you up?' I asked.

'Yeah, go on then,' she replied.

'Ok, well, Tim who I met yesterday and Rod went to the first ever twin town meeting in Huelgoat,' I started excitedly. 'Tim was better with French so got volunteered to become a committee member. Once they'd picked him, they took him downstairs to choose his role in some weird ritual. He's now treasurer. All that means is he organises the occasional meeting and event.'

'Like what?' asked RG.

'This year they're trying to set up a football match between the towns. St Just has a team ready to come over but Huelgoat can't find enough players. Just a few old men. So Tim's not sure what's going to happen.'

'I like Roscoff,' said RG, munching her sandwich. 'It reminds me of Falmouth. The boats, the smiley people...'

'Ok, so, well, if you thought that was a great story, wait for *this* one... Tim once took a bunch of Bretons to Cornwall as part of the new twinning relationship between Huelgoat and St Just. Bit of a road trip.'

'Ok,' said RG, examining her sandwich.

'He told me most of the story with a cheeky grin and with Amanda, his wife, chipping in from the kitchen and reminding him about bits. At one point on the journey to St Just, while Tim was driving the coach, one of the group started stuffing marshmallows into his mouth. Oh and then—'

'Such a pretty little town,' said RG. 'Just a shame about the bloody weather.'

'On their last night, they had a party,' I continued. 'Everyone had a drink – the Brits a bit too much to the surprise of some of the Bretons. But, being Breton, they soon joined in. There was lots of banter. Then the Bretons played a trick on their hosts and of course as the only person who could translate Tim had to be involved.'

'Let's walk down here,' said RG, spotting a cobbled alley off Rue Amiral Réveillère. 'While we do, tell me what happened to the Cornish.'

I followed RG towards the coast. 'Ah – so you *are* listening.'

'Always. Just multitasking. I can walk, talk, eat *and* listen.'

'I learn something new about you every day,' I said, pulling back her hood for a kiss. 'So, one of the Bretons phoned Tim, who had to pretend he was speaking to the ferry company. The ferry was cancelled due to bad weather, or so they pretended. So during this evening of heavy drinking and fun, poor Tim had to announce to everyone that the French would be staying another night.

'The Cornish started dashing around, trying to find accommodation for 20 Bretons. They called hotels and friends. They were trying everyone to find a bed for their stranded guests.'

'That's terrible,' said RG. 'The poor Bretons.'

'But it was a hoax, lady,' I said. 'The ferry hadn't been cancelled. There *was* no phonecall, except from the Breton bloke. Tim had to make it all up on the spot. Wicked sense of humour – that's something Tim said he's noticed about the Cornish and Bretons.'

Checking the Roscoff website, we discovered a fair bit happening between Great Torrington and its twin. Like Huelgoat, Roscoff had a big organising committee, comprising lots of people with names like Jean-Jacques and Michel. Back in 2009, a group representing Great Torrington had taken the ferry to Roscoff to celebrate 35 years of friendship between the towns. Parties and get-togethers went on from Saturday to Monday.

We strolled along the pebbled beach and back into town. There we spotted a tiny restaurant where the chef 'proposes you real dishes Home-Made, Completely Elaborated in our Kitchen...', which sounded delightful. A poster told us there was an Indian-Bretagne dance festival called 'Tillana Tillana' coming to Roscoff. And a plaque near the town's restaurants helped me make sense of Amanda's onion comment.

It was in a house in Roscoff in 1869 that Alexandre Dumas, author of *The Count of Monte Cristo* and *The Three Musketeers*, wrote his other great work: the onion chapter of his *Grand Dictionnaire de Cuisine*. Why Roscoff? Because it was the *oignon* capital of France at the time, of course. And as every good writer knows, '*Si pour bien parler d'un sujet, il faut avoir ce sujet sous les yeu,*' or, 'If you're going to write about something, you need to see it yourself.'

My favourite tale from Dumas' onion book is about a Breton called Monsieur Corbière who, in the early 19th century, took a boat to England to tell the English about Brittany's lovely onions.

'THE ENGLISH ONION IS NOT GOOD,' he wrote on a giant placard that he erected in the middle of London. Below, he put a cart of French onions.

Monsieur Corbière apparently got into a fight, which, according to Dumas, he won with ease, taking his combatant by the shirt collar and wrestling him to the ground. The battle was over. The French onion had, again according to a slightly biased, onion-loving Dumas, conquered England.

'That's the sort of war I'm ok with,' I said as we queued for some fries.

'I'm ok with Roscoff,' said RG. 'Just wish this rain would stop. It's really cramping my style, y'know?'

Rob

Hi Rob

Douarnanez has quite a lot in common with Falmouth –
popular port for yachties, some nice little town beaches
– but also some interesting contrasts. It's maybe a bit
like Falmouth would have been without the university.

There's a link with the artist Christopher Wood, who
painted quite a lot in the area as well as in Cornwall. We
went there for that reason (my wife was writing a book on
Wood) and visited a beautiful fisherman's church that Wood
painted in the 20s. Don't really know anything about what
the 'twinning' means in practice, though.

All best,

Tom

10 · Douarnenez Twinned with Falmouth

—

In which things get fishy

Dear Tom

Socialist revolution, women's rights and an attempted assassination. Who would've thought a small, unassuming coastal town like Douarnenez was capable of such a history? From your email, you perhaps.

The image your message had conjured in our minds came to life as we drove along the coast and into Douarnenez, our third Breton twin. There was the port with its bobbing yachts, a row of colourful buildings, and then the rest of the town perched haphazardly on a hill. We parked on a sloping street and, as we left the car, bowed our heads away from the pouring rain.

If this had been Falmouth, students would have been heading home from a lecture, or perhaps we'd have spotted a family of holidaymakers ducking into a pub. But with no university and no tourists, the streets of Douarnenez were eerily quiet.

'Nothing's open. There's no-one around. We might as well go and find some lunch,' said RG, matter-of-factly. 'Maybe we can get chatting to someone there.'

An information board had caught my attention. 'There's a walking trail here,' I shouted through the rain. 'Let's do it. Just don't lead us the wrong direction like you did in Cormeilles, ok?'

I could hear RG's stomach groan as the rain dripped from our hoods. 'Let's go and find somewhere to have lunch first,' she prodded, 'and we'll see if we come across any other clues on the way. K?'

As I turned to tell my travelling companion it sounded like a decent plan, I watched her do the splits on a slippery bronze circle. I reached out just in time to stop her face rendezvousing with the pavement.

'Let's head down this hill. Bet it leads to the water and somewhere to eat.'

The downhill roads of Falmouth – I remember from my time studying your course in the town – always led to either the docks or the sea. And it was the same in your twin town. The cobbled slope I'd spotted led us down to a sloshy and moody Atlantic. There the sea was slapping the harbour walls and wind was whipping noisily around the waterfront shops and restaurants.

We soon stumbled across another information board. But by now RG's hunger had pushed her away from me and towards a shop window display of sardine tins. There were tins everywhere, in different shapes, colours and designs.

'Can't you just imagine Jerry tucking himself into one to evade Tom?' RG shouted from the distance.

'Yeah. Hey, this info board thing is called The Sardine Itinerary,' I shouted back through sheets of rain. 'Turns out Douarnenez is a big sardine fishing town. The walk starts on Plomar'ch. Where's Plomar'ch?'

We soon learnt how every year, from the beginning of summer, sardines swim up the Bay of Biscay and pour into the bay of Douarnenez in their millions. For centuries, the fishing and processing of this small silvery blue fish has been the main product of the town's maritime community.

Douarnenez's fishy history goes back 2000 years, we found out, when Gallo-Romans put up a massive garum factory. Garum became a popular sauce, made from fermented fish and salt. As centuries passed, Douarnenez's fishing industry grew. By the 19th century, the town was canning their sardines to preserve them. Around this time, your twin was the largest sardine exporter in the world.

'Does it say where to find the next board?' RG asked.

'I think we just guess,' I guessed.

Sardines were a currency for Douarnenez's locals. They were people's lives, from fishermen to factory women. This meant times were perilous during the so-called 'Sardine Crisis' of the 20th century. Brittany's fishermen just couldn't catch enough to make a good living. But why? Were the fish keeping at deeper levels, out of reach of the Breton fishermen? Were there problems with the cod roe bait? Perhaps the nets weren't good enough? Nobody was sure. But the crisis was big enough to make Canada's *Montreal Gazette*. Perhaps an international twin town for the future?

Reading the boards, we learnt how miserable the early 20th century was for the people of small fishing towns. Something had to happen to put smiles back on faces. And that something was a man called Jacques de Thezac.

Thezac built *L'Abri du Marin* (Sailors' Homes) as refuges for soul-searching fishermen who'd turned to alcohol to escape their lives. These were designed to be a clean-cut alternative to bars and cabarets. They served eucalyptus infusions instead of booze, and sailors would play wholesome games as opposed to gambling. Imagine it – rehabilitated sailors politely sipping herbal tea and playing a civilised game of billiards.

A great pink building stands defiantly, alone, against the unforgiving port weather in Douarnenez. During our visit, it housed the local maritime magazine *Chasse Marée*, but it was once the town's *L'Abri du Marin*. Its pinkness was a characteristic of all twelve refuges that went up around Brittany in the first half of the century.

By 1924, the working class people of Douarnenez were starting to rise up against poor wages and bad working conditions. At the end of the year, it was time for the *penn sardin*, the factory women, to be taken seriously. For generations, these women had worked long hours in stinking canning factories for basically nothing. By November 1924, they'd had enough. Three thousand women went on strike to demand better wages. The information board displayed a black-and-white photo of the marchers – their hardened faces showed they meant business.

By early afternoon, the rain had stopped just long enough for us to slip off our hoods and take in the full breadth of the port.

'You can just imagine them here, can't you?' RG said to me, looking proud as she took in the length of the bay. 'Thousands of women, marching and chanting for their rights. It must've been massively emotional. I love it.'

For the 48 days of the strike, the women had support from the national press and emerging communist party. Douarnenez was no longer just a fishing town – it was a symbol for the struggling lower classes. The strike ended after the attempted assassination of one of the strike leaders, Daniel le Flanchec. Le Flanchec was also the communist mayor of the town.

'Cor, that's quite a bit of drama,' I heard RG growl enthusiastically. 'Who would've thought it? Other than your Tom.'

We eventually found an overpriced restaurant along the bay. The local newspaper told us to look out for rain, storms and possibly some rainstorms. It was all too familiar. But it felt silly to complain when not long before people here had been fighting for their livelihoods.

'That's coming up for 100 years ago,' I said to RG over haché. 'Strikes, revolution, communism. Seems like a world away. Except for the rallies in Paris and Nazi sites in Germany and terrorism in...'

Douarnenez remained one of the biggest canners in Europe. But two wars and competition from Spain and Portugal spoilt its sardine canning monopoly. The town had to adapt and evolve over the years.

One of the few constants in Douarnenez's history was religion. We found no bigger testament to that than the magnificent church you mentioned in your message, the Sacre Coeur. The designer had intertwined typical Christian imagery and scenes of men at sea in the stained-glass windows and door sculpting. This church had once had the power to bring everyone in the town together – for celebration, for prayer and for mourning men lost at sea.

From the final information board we learnt Douarnenez was known as the 'red town' because it was at the heart of the French socialist movement.

'Rod told us France, or at least Brittany, is still full of socialist sensibilities,' said RG. 'He said people will quite happily give a homeless person some change because there's still a sense of helping each other out.'

Our time in Douarnenez was almost up. But before we left, we discovered how to properly find your way along the trail. The answer had been staring us in the face all along – in fact, it'd almost smashed RG in the face. That bronze circle in the ground she'd slipped on? It'd had an imprint of a fish on it – a sardine. There was one at every board and each faced the way we should've gone next.

'We're idiots,' I said, standing by the first board, but the last on our tour.

'Idiots with a load of new knowledge at least,' said RG, taking me by the soggy arm.

Rob

Hello Rob

I'm interested in Benodet which is in Brittany. It's twinned with Torpoint in Cornwall where my wife's dad lives. I drove through it once on holiday. It seemed nice. Torpoint, on the other hand, is a shit-hole.

Good Luck, Andy

11 · Benodet
Twinned with Torpoint
—

In which nothing seems to make sense

Dear Andy

Half-naked women everywhere. Bronzed, half-naked women laying back on soft, golden sand. Sapphire sea ahead of them, a few tiny beach huts behind them nestled in lush shrubbery and woodland. A dolphin leaping from the water and arching gracefully for re-entry. What a view.

What a view the photographer who took that photo of Benodet must've had that sunny morning – the photo on the postcard RG had just picked up in the souvenir shop on the seafront. We'd ducked into the store, which also stocked bats and balls and buckets and spades and kites, because the weather had turned so bloody awful outside. When would it stop?

You said you'd been through Benodet once and it'd looked nice. Unlike its twin Torpoint, which was a 'shit-hole'. Well today, with the weather as it was, most visitors to Benodet would've given your twin the description you gave Torpoint. But not a couple of hardy twin town folk like me and RG. Oh no. By now, we were made of harder, less absorbent stuff.

We didn't need beaches full of perfect bodies to enjoy a little coastal town in Brittany. We just needed a couple of stories from leathery locals to bring the place to life. The problem was, on a day like today, with the wind screaming and rain stinging, even the Bretons were staying indoors.

Before we had any idea Benodet even *had* a seafront, we'd pulled up in what looked like a public car park near the tourist information office.

'Where's Torpoint?' RG asked me, getting out of the car.

'On the Tamar I think, in Cornwall, but near Devon. According to Andy, it's... not very nice. It's where his wife's dad lives.'

'Let's hope its twin's a bit better then,' said RG, wrapping up in her waterproof once again.

Returning to KT after popping into the tourist information, we realised it wasn't a public car park after all. It was the grounds of a school. Which explained why so many young boys were pointing at my car through the windows. And why the big, hairy teacher man inside had wagged his finger at us.

Caroline in the tourist information hadn't told us much. She'd had no leaflets, no stories, no knowledge of England, no twinning tales and was aching to lock up and clear off.

'Have you seen here?' she'd said, circling a fan-like symbol on a map. 'It is a good view of the coast. There is a path. Visit here. Have good fun. Good evening.'

'*Centre ville?*' RG had asked.

'There is a path. Good evening.'

'To the town?' I'd asked.

'There is no town. Not really. Good evening.'

Not really? Not really a town? Or was Caroline just joking – *of course there's a town, you foolish Brits, I'm just pulling your leg.* We headed straight to the symbol to take in the view. Then I was determined to find the town.

On the short drive, a few raindrops hit the windscreen but nothing more.

We laughed at these raindrops. They were the feckless younger siblings of Cormeille's hailstones and Douarnenez's wall of rain. They fell half-heartedly, almost expecting KT to just brush them aside with a flick of her wrist.

'*Pathétique*,' I said to RG. 'Seems it's drying up. Turning, perhaps. Finally.'

We did a little high five.

KT stayed in the car park while RG and I – wrapped in now-slightly-less-than-waterproof waterproofs – headed down a gravel track towards the sea. A lady coming towards us with her dog shook her head as we passed. We smiled and *bonjoured*.

'I think a scowl is as good as a smile to the French,' I said to RG.

The coast ended a few feet ahead of us. It became a choppy, murky, mucky sea soup. Spray lifted from it, from right to left. But on land it was still dry and full of beautiful views, if you like clouds.

Although I don't know Torpoint, I've walked along a lot of Cornish coast – from Falmouth's Gyllyngvase Beach to Maenporth, from Lizard Head to Kynance Cove, along the cliffs at Bossiney. During my two years' living in the South West, lost weekends of walking were my favourites. So looking out towards the Atlantic today, enormous waves lifting windsurfers frightening distances from the surf, I felt right at home.

'Shall we go for a walk?' I asked RG. 'Bet it's lovely in the town.'

'There is no town,' said RG, rooted to the spot. 'Not really.'

Five minutes into the walk, the sea disappeared. To our left, there was now a loud, whistling, misty sort of nothingness. Wind was blowing all kinds of wet-ness out of that nothingness and into our faces.

A week before we set off for France, we'd been half-planning the trip (aka snog-ging) in my parents' garden. The scorching early-spring sunshine had persuad-ed us to invest in factor-50 suncream. Afternoons on the glimmering Thames had us dreaming of lost afternoons drinking red wine outside cute French cafés and devouring crêpes. Instead, we were dressed in winter jumpers, coats and waterproofs, our clothes were starting to smell of damp and grow moss, and we were spending most afternoons fighting gales and rainstorms. The suncream, we'd concluded, would probably never meet the sun.

'At least we have each other,' we'd started to say to each other. A lot.

By the time we'd reached the beach hut and salivated a little at the sunny scenes on the postcards, our clothes were sodden. With windburnt faces, we sat for a *thé au lait* and cappuccino in a café.

'So, Brittany. Very much like Cornwall. That's what I've spotted so far,' I said to RG, trying to avoid another weather conversation. 'It seems to have its own personality. I mean it feels nothing like Paris or Cormeilles or Albert.'

'I agree,' said RG. 'Nice that we can make those comparisons.'

'The locals seem to be friendly, too – and quite a few of them are Brits.'

'Yep,' said RG. 'And it's beautiful, with the hills and little villages and cobbled streets. Shame about the w-word.'

'Agreed. Brittany good, w-word bad,' I concluded, cradling my tea like it was a Cup-a-Soup and I was a pensioner.

'Tell you what's really fascinating me,' I went on. 'The Celtic connection. The Breton language looks and sounds like Cornish, from what I know of it, which is very little. And do you remember what Skye was saying about it?'

'Last night at dinner?' said RG. 'Yep.'

'Cool. What did she say? I can't remember the details.'

RG reminded me that Skye (Mel and Rod's pre-teen daughter) had told us all about the Breton language over dinner the night before. Like Cornish, the language wasn't spoken by many people any more. Schools were trying to keep the flame flickering by giving classes, but with French now de rigeur and English spoken by the numerous expats, they had a battle on their hands.

A sticker was stuck to the inside of the café window in Benodet. Around the word 'Celt' there were flags for the following places:

Breizh (Bretagne)
Alba (Ecosse)
Eire (Irlande)
Wales (Pays de Galles)
Galiza (Galice)
Cornwall (Cornouilles)
Mannin (Ile de Man)

'There's something strange going on,' I said to RG, picking at the sticker. 'What's the connection?'

We'd seen on the Breton road signs – and heard from Skye – that Cornwall and Brittany had similar-looking second languages. And we'd learnt from Rod's book on Brittany how the Brits had left Britain in the 4th century to start life again on the north coast of France.

'But there must be so much more that connects these places,' I said to RG, buttoning up for the walk back to the car.

'The Gauls, gallic, Pays de Galles. What about those?' she added.

'And the Brecon Beacons and Bretons? Ok, maybe not that. But Cornish often looks Welsh. And the number of times I've heard a Scottish person speak and confused them for someone Irish. There's some sort of national connection here, lady, and town twinning's right in the middle of it.'

Benodet, rather than just a damp squib, had opened up a world of intrigue. Even if it didn't have a town centre.

On the walk back to the car, more questions bashed into one another in my head. The biggest was this: *how on earth are we going to answer all these questions about shared identities with just one Breton twin to go?*

Then it came to me. I'd had an idea that might just change the course of history. Or at least give us something to do in Lorient.

Rob

Rob

I was going to suggest that Wirral is twinned with an area in France, so that might interest you. If I remember correctly, it's twinned with Gennevilliers and Lorient (I might have spelled the first one wrong).

If I had to choose, I'd say Lorient. I like the sound of Brittany.

Speak soon! Roz

12 · Lorient
Twinned with the Wirral

—

In which some things start to make sense

Dear Roz

'It's simple,' I said to RG. 'We leave England. We leave England and set up life in Brittany. I've already lived in Cornwall, so I'm kind of used to this way of living. You visited me a couple of times in Falmouth, twinned with Douarnenez, so you sort of know it. We like Mel and Rod, and Tim and Amanda are nice, which will make the move easier. Yep, when we get to Lorient, let's start looking for a place.'

RG was driving. It didn't look like she was listening.

'Let's move to Brittany,' I repeated. 'Are you listening?'

She seemed to think about it as we narrowly avoided driving the wrong way down a one-way street, then said, 'Nah. It's lovely but... nah. It's always raining and that means I can't stop sneezing. I prefer sunshine.'

And that was it. The end of my idea that might just change the course of history. I returned to simpler, more realistic pursuits – like trying to find out as much as I could about the European Celtic connection.

Galicia. That was the one that was bothering me. I could now join Cornwall and Brittany in my head, and Cornwall and Wales, and Wales, Scotland, Ireland and the Isle of Man. But Galicia?

So far in Brittany, we'd got an overwhelming feeling of middle age and old age – families with a couple of teenagers who'd probably gone off to uni, and white-haired folk with a couple of walking sticks. In Lorient, for the first time, we were surrounded by teens chatting and shouting and chasing and giggling and smoking. Boys and girls dressed like models in vintage clothes, strolling the streets, smoking like chimneys.

It made sense when we realised we'd just parked outside a college.

'Right, let's split up,' I said to RG, putting my arm around her shoulder.

'What?' said RG. 'But everything's going well. I get a bit tired now and then and I don't like the rain, and your moving to Brittany idea was silly, but... Is it because I've parked outside a college and it makes you feel old? I'm sorry...'

I realised what I'd said. 'No, silly. I'll go to the town hall, you go to the tourist information. That sort of splitting up.'

RG smiled. 'Ohhhh, I knew that. Deal. Divide and conquer.' And off she went.

The *hotel de ville* of Lorient was a large, clinical building – a bit like the one where we'd found Sébastien back in Issy-les-Moulineaux. Outside on the large, clinical paved square, I spotted a fingerpost. One finger read:

The Wirral, 618km

The sun was shining and full of springtime heat. People were pouring onto the streets. Inside the town hall, I tried the usual line about *jumelage* and my *projet* but got nothing except an instruction to *descendre* some *escaliers* for the Relations Internationales et Jumelages. Intrigued, I headed down some steps and walked out into yet another featureless square.

An African couple passed me and smiled. Ahead, a tiny blonde lady stood before another charmless civic building. With blue skies overhead and a quest in my heart, Lorient took on a serenity.

I reached an intercom and pushed the button. Something buzzed. A distant French girl said lots of words. I said, *'Parlez-vous Anglais?'* She said, *'Non.'* I said, 'Oh.' She said more words. I froze. Then, just as I was about to run away crying, a blonde lady who'd gone inside the building a few minutes earlier came back out. I nipped in as the door was closing and started looking for clues about twinning.

I struck gold at the first attempt and met Christine.

'I don't have much but I can tell you something,' she said, her big hair curling dramatically away from her head. 'I am the representation of town twinning here in Lorient.'

I asked her how strong Lorient's relationship with the Wirral was. She shook her head, shrugged her broad shoulders and sighed. 'Not good. It is hard. You do not make the town twinning easy.'

It seemed us Brits, or at least the people of your hometown, weren't doing well at twinning. Back in 1957, the mayors of Lorient and Bebington, a little town on the Wirral you might know, signed charters making their friendship official. But since then, as Lorient has twinned with towns across Europe, including Galway in Ireland, the relationship has faded. However, Lorient's other relationships have got stronger.

'Because the Wirral has a new may-jor every year it is difficult,' Christine told me, speaking as though she had all the time in the world. 'Also, it is more difficult with the schools. A lot of families will like children from the Wirral to visit but it is hard to finding families in the Wirral for the children here.

'But Galway is strong. Two years before now, we celebrate 35 years.'

Christine went on to tell me how Lorient was almost completely destroyed during the second world war. The Germans had built a U-boat base here in 1940, having captured the city earlier that year. By 1943, there were up to 28

U-boats at the base. A hugely important site to the war effort, the Nazis defended it with all they had. But by August 1944, German forces were starting to lose their grip on the city. American soldiers, who in June had landed at Normandy (about 50 miles from Michel and Chantal's Cormeilles), had reached the outskirts. By the end of the war, around 30 Allied bombing raids had flattened 90% of Lorient's houses.

If only Lorient's and the Wirral's relationship were as strong as the German resistance and Allied resolve, I thought as I crossed the busy shopping street that led to the city centre and luscious central park.

Outside the featureless mall, I spotted RG waiting in the sunshine with a grin.

'You found something?' I asked.

She looked up. 'Sunshine. And it's pretty darn warm. Look.' She pointed to her bare shoulders, glistening like salted caramel.

'And the tourist info?' I asked.

'Yep,' she said, still beaming.

'Cool. You look excited. What?'

'It's lunchtime so it's shut,' she said. 'But look up. Sunshine!'

'Bugger. I mean yay, but bugger.'

I'd been lucky. Christine, I now realised, had been on lunch when I'd let myself into her office and offered myself a seat. While she'd regaled me with tales of old Lorient and it's near extinction, she should have been strolling around the city with a baguette under her arm.

'You know everything's shut at lunchtime,' said RG. 'I've just been wandering around the city, sussing it out, taking in the rays. The park's lovely. And it looks cool around the harbour. Cool and hot, y'know.'

We started to wander through the warm, spring sunshine.

According to a flyer for the Festival Interceltique de Lorient I'd picked up from the ground, Lorient had hosted an annual international Celtic festival since 1971. People with Celtic heritage would come from all over the world to celebrate their roots – from Cornwall, Scotland, Wales, Ireland, the Isle of Man and, of course, Galicia.

Galicia, it turned out, was an area in northwest Spain. The Celts, or Britons – a frightening bunch who'd made their way around Europe for thousands of years before Christ – spent a lot of time there. One or more Celtic tribes (nobody's quite sure how many) arrived in the area around 500BC. Art work and engravings discovered there matched almost exactly with those found in rock formations in Ireland, confirming the connection.

According to galiciaguide.com, Galicia was known as 'green Spain', thanks to its temperate climate and amount of rain fall. That made it a close sibling of all those other lush places on the sticker in Benodet, especially soaked and sodden Bretagne.

'They really got around,' said RG, wrapping up a little in the sharp sea breeze. 'Bit like us, innit.'

There was just enough time to take a stroll along Quai de Rohan and look out in the general direction of the German U-boat 'dom' bunkers from L'Estacade. With the sun twinkling on the water, and fishing boat bells tinkling in the distance, Lorient again took on an air of serenity.

Rob

Rob,

This sounds like fun.

Frome, my nearest town, has three twins:

Château-Gontier in France,
Murrhardt in Germany,
Rabka-Zdrój in Poland.

Don't really know anything about any of them but
presumably the first has a castle of some kind.
Find out for me?

Bon voyage.

Ben

13 · Château-Gontier
Twinned with Frome
—

In which a very important man is missing

Dear Ben

Leaving Brittany hurt. We'd bonded in the short time I'd been in its undulating greenness. I'd felt like an old Englander and ex-Cornishman, leaving Celtic Cornouailles for a new start on the north coast of France. But there was no new start and no time to relax. Just 13 twins and two weeks into the adventure, reality was telling us to get a move on.

'Two and a half months to visit another 32 twins,' I said to RG, as we drove south through fields of glorious, glowing rapeseed. 'That's a twin every couple of days. Easy, I'd say. Well, doable.'

'Easy in Brittany,' said RG, blocking half the windscreen with another stupendously oversized roadmap Mel and Rod had donated. 'Not so easy when you think soon we have to look around Poitiers in France and Porto in Portugal in two days. Have you seen how far the drive is?'

Not long after the glowing fields, we discovered the ugly, soulless, industrial estates of France. These seemed to fill the spaces between any two towns with beautiful names.

'Tell you what I'm looking forward to,' I said to RG, remembering to go the wrong way around the roundabouts. 'A chateau. As nice and jumpable as Marly's foundations were, I bet the castle would've been better.'

We reached your twin at dusk and drove down a long, straight, tree-lined street.

L'office de tourisme was closed so we parked outside a supermarket where some boys were urinating and wandered back between the trees to find a hotel. Then we walked back along the same street again, past banks, insurance firms, a homemade jewellery shop and some elderly people peeking at us through their windows. We ended up staying in a pricey hotel-bar about fifty yards from the weeing teens.

RG decided to eat the previous night's leftovers again. I couldn't think of anything worse so headed into town to locate some delicious local cuisine.

'Don't you dare find the chateau,' warned RG, as I put on my coat. 'I want to find it with you, ok?'

'Ok.' We kissed goodbye.

The evening had turned chillier. And KT had made a new friend in the car park – an ancient Citroën. It was white, dented and very scratched. As I strolled past, I gritted my teeth at the thought of some little old Frenchman opening a door into KT's side. Just as I reached the water at the bottom of the hill, I heard a door-dinking bang behind me, then an engine start. I turned to see a little old man driving the Citroën away. My fear had become reality. I may have cried a little.

Across the river, a building shone golden in the final rays of the day. It was a wondrous piece of architecture, stretching along the bank, its windows bright like silver teeth. Too excited to find real food, I grabbed a *kebab et frites* and dashed back to the hotel through steep cobbled streets.

I sent RG a text from the bar. 'Come downstairs. I have good news x'

RG replied immediately. 'Great. I hope it's not that you found the chateau x'

'Um. No. I'm eating a kebab x'

The next morning, we rose early. I felt like a child at Christmas, too excited to sleep. At the bridge crossing La Mayenne river, I pointed to the building I'd seen the night before. It was tall and wide with sloping roofs and creamy orange walls full of windows.

'That looks like a nice building,' I said to RG. 'And it's the first time I've seen it. With you. At this moment. What do you think?'

'About what?' she asked.

'Château-Gontier's chateau,' I said, pointing and grinning.

'You think that's it?' asked RG. 'Doesn't look very... castle-y. It's got millions of windows and sloping roofs and it's not up high. Castles are usually high up on hills and more... castle-y. That looks more like, I dunno, a hospital?'

'Why can't you ever just admit I'm right?' I said. 'It's obviously a chateau. Look at it. It couldn't be more castle-y if it tried.'

There was only one way to confirm my certainty.

'The chateau?' laughed the lady behind the desk at the tourist office. 'That's funny about this town. There is no chateau. No more. It's gone.'

'Gone where?' I asked.

'Taken down a long time ago. There is no chateau no more in Château-Gontier.' She laughed again.

RG giggled with her. 'That's funny.' She looked across to me and touched my hand. 'Funny, isn't it, Rob?'

'Very,' I said. 'Very funny indeed.'

I picked up a map of the town from the mean lady's desk. 'But the building beside the river? The beautiful building. It looks like kings and queens would have lived there. Sure that's not the castle?'

The pretty building on La Mayenne was, as RG had guessed, a hospital. The castle – much like the castle at Marly-le-Roi – had disappeared long before we turned up. It had once perched above the river to protect the region against invaders, including the Bretons of Brittany. But no longer.

In just a few centuries, this part of La Mayenne grew from a small fort and defensive tower into a bustling town. The castle, sadly, didn't survive. Between them, the French and the English managed to destroy it – the French removing numerous city walls and castles around the country in an attempt to stop any collective force rebelling against its king.

The hospital, on the other hand, was still there – and bloody lovely, too. As was Couvent des Ursulines, the convent which housed the tourist information centre. We had a stroll around the cloisters (and up a staircase that led to nothing but embarrassment as we had to walk back down past the people who clearly knew it led to nothing) before I had a brainwave.

'Let's find the castle,' I said to RG.

'Do you *ever* listen, Rob?' she replied, giving me a faux-slap around the ear.

'I know the woman said there isn't one, but haven't we learnt there's usually *some* part of old things left? It'd still be cool to at least stand in the spot where the castle stood a thousand years ago.'

The lady back in the tourist office confirmed we could still walk to the site of the old castle. And if we went on from there along Rue Trehut, she added, we'd soon come to the house of Monsieur Cadoret, president of the Comité de Jumelage et d'Echanges Internationaux. Perfect.

Near the church of St Jean Baptiste, we found a view that a guardsman on the ramparts of the old castle might have looked out to. Through nettles, we could see the pastels of the shops and offices behind the river, which looked like a Mars milkshake, and the dome of the hospital to the right.

We walked and walked and walked. Clouds came across and blocked the warm sunshine, then floated away again on a strengthening breeze. We wandered around a cemetery. Then, after what seemed like hours of plodding, we found the road we needed. And then the house we needed.

'*Monsieur Cadoret – il est ici?*' I asked two clean-shaven workmen.

The thinner, darker-haired man shouted downstairs. 'Monsieur Cadoret?'

The men shook their heads, apologised and continued their work. We shrugged and walked away from the house where the man involved in Château-Gontier's twinning with Frome from the beginning lived.

There was only one thing that could make me feel better.

Your twin, according to its town sign, was known for its flowers and gardens. There was even a Frome Garden somewhere along La Mayenne. But, of course, we didn't find that. We instead reached the pretty Jardin des Senteurs, where a fierce wind was whipping lemon smells through the air.

I reclined and thought about our two weeks of travelling. It'd been lovely. Nothing huge had happened, but it'd been lovely. Nice. Really nice. Pleasant, even. Everything was going smoothly and I was bored with the lack of drama.

'It's citronella,' shouted RG, bounding up to me with a wide, childlike smile. 'Oh dear. What's wrong?'

Rob

Rob

I live in Lewes, which is twinned with a beautiful looking French town called Blois. It's got everything: a chateau, a history of Nazi occupation and a completely unfathomable pronunciation.

Nick

14 · Blois
Twinned with Lewes

—

In which major doubts rear their ugly heads

Dear Nick

'B-L-O-I-S,' I spelt out to RG as we turned yet another corner into yet another confusing one-way part of your twin town. 'B-L-O-I-S. Blow-ee.'

'It can't be Blow-ee,' said RG, shaking her head. 'O-I-S isn't ever pronounced 'ee' in French. Plus I'm sure a blow-ee is slang for something that's very not a twin town in the middle of France. Must be *Blue-wah*.'

It was evening – big shadows and constant drizzle were turning every second sunlit street into a deathtrap. We took another left onto a road we'd just seen.

'We're going round in circles,' I whined to my travelling companion.

'I know,' said RG.

'Well can you stop us doing that?' I said.

'No. I don't know where we are. Why can't we just get the bloody satnav working?'

'Because the bloody satnav's bloody rubbish and I need you to help me get to the hotel so I can stop driving round in bloody circles and breathe.'

RG went silent.

'Fine,' I said, 'I'll work it out myself.' We stopped at a junction. 'I'll go left here.'

This is roughly how our first navigation bust-up went – though we may have been a little more creative with the bloodys. This wasn't the drama I was after. Neither was turning out of a one-way system back onto a normal road and heading down a hill on the wrong side.

'Rob?'

'I know,' I said. 'I'm on the left and there's a car coming towards us. It's fine.'

I could see RG staring at me. 'ROB?'

Ten minutes later we were sitting in KT about a five-minute walk from our hotel. My eyes were closed and my shoulders shaking. Just before we'd gone too far down the hill, two cars had pulled up sharply to let us cut back onto the right-hand lane. We were lucky. While breaking the law, we'd spotted our hotel on a corner at the next junction. It was small, dark and sinister-looking.

Inside, the landlord insisted on speaking to us in French. We guessed he was telling us that we didn't have a room booked. There was *'une problème'*. Five minutes later, we'd learnt it wasn't a particularly *grande problème*, as he still had rooms available. It was just our booking.com confirmation hadn't ever reached him.

The next morning, RG decided to ask the landlord what to do in Blow-ee to get the best Blow-ee experience. We understood just two words of his response.

'Ah, so it *is* pronounced Blue-wah,' RG said to the man, turning to me and touching my hand. 'That's funny, isn't it, Rob?'

'Very,' I said, sick of getting things wrong. 'Very funny indeed.'

The other word we heard was 'chateau'.

'Let's do it,' said RG. 'The chateau. I really want to see a chateau now, after Marly and Chateau-Gonts.'

'I'd love to, but I need to do some twin town stuff,' I replied. 'I don't feel like I'm getting any further with the twinnings. Lots of these relationships just seem random – like two towns have been drawn from a hat and plonked together. Or it's about business, like in Paris. Where's the heart gone, lady? Maybe we're just not seeing the heart.'

At Place Victor Hugo, a little distracted by the ornate architecture towering above, I managed to jump out of the way of two thick, wide, determined horses. They were charging past, pulling behind them a cart full of tiny French children and their parents. We followed the excited gasps up Rue de la Voûte Chateau and within a couple of minutes had reached the Chateau Royal.

'Shall we?' I asked RG.

'But what about all the stuff you just said about town twinning – not knowing enough, needing to find more stories, getting to the heart?'

'I know, I know. That's all really important. But I like horses. Please?'

Then, unless I'm mistaken, one of the horses looked at me and smiled.

We bought two tickets for Balade en attelage dans l'historie de Blois and sat back. While our friendly horses gave us the tour of your twin, and the tour guide spoke in a language I'd proved I could spout in spurts but not understand, I did as much research as I could from my phone. According to completefrance.com, the relationship between Lewes and Blois was a very healthy one. It started in 1963 as an official partnership, though the first school exchange was in 1947. An educational report from that year highlighted the importance of introducing children to other ways of living. The Clarke Report, the first report produced by the Central Advisory Councils for Education, concluded that: 'There are certain ways in which the school can meet children's needs as even the good home cannot: e.g. through nursery schools, through playing fields, camps, visits and journeys abroad'.

So the 1947 school exchange between Lewes and Blois wasn't unique, but it was certainly a catalyst for greater things between your twin and hometown. While bumping through the picturesque old streets of the town and taking in bottom smells of two giant, blinkered horses, I emailed Jackie, the chair of the Lewes Twinning Association, and asked her about the 1947 exchange.

'I spotted a cool-looking café down one of these streets,' said RG, wobbling a little after our journey through town. 'It had a top hat in the window. And books. Let's eat there.'

Within five minutes, the top hat was on RG's head and I was sipping a pint that tasted oddly like colon.

'It's a beautiful town,' said RG, doing her best Marlene Dietrich impression. 'Going along the Loire then up Rue Denis Papin was incredible. So pretty, especially when the sun came out.'

I said nothing.

'I bet all the information the smiley horse lady was giving was really interesting too. If only we spoke French eh?'

'If only we were better Europeans,' I said, feeling dejected.

As we started our walk around Chateau de Blois, I tried to organise my memories and tell myself it was natural to feel a little overwhelmed by everything we'd seen and done. We'd visited 14 towns in two weeks, driven over a thousand miles, met a dozen new people, learnt thousands of years of history. And yet town twinning, and Europe, was still a mystery to me.

'My head hurts,' I whispered to RG, as we took in some of the 35,000 works of art inside the chateau.

'Did you read the chateau was designed by Francois Mansart?' she replied. 'Wasn't Marly-le-Roi designed by someone called Mansart? All these little connections. I love it.'

Jules Hardouin-Mansart, the architect behind Louis XIV's grand getaway in Marly, was great-nephew of Francois Mansart. Francois's biggest claim to architectural fame was the mansard roof – a double-sloping roof design, popular in the mid-19th century. Though he did so much more.

In the early 17th century, another Louis – Louis VIII – became the absolute ruler of France, overthrowing the many papal kingdoms of the country (like Bretagne and Normandie). With one ruler, there was less need for fortified castles. Many were taken down, like in Château-Gontier. While new chateaux, commissioned by the French nobility, focused more on aesthetics than defences. Architects like Francois Mansart thrived. They began incorporating gardens and ponds in their designs, like those RG and I had marvelled at in the grounds of Marly-le-Roi.

With over 500 rooms and a mixture of classic, renaissance and gothic architecture, it would be easy to lose days in the Chateau Royal. But with every creaking step, I felt more like a twin town fraud.

'Do you think we're doing this properly?' asked RG, as we packed KT's boot with scientific accuracy back at the hotel. 'We still don't really know about Blois and Lewes. What are we going to tell Nick – that you drank colon beer, I wore a top hat and we stayed in a dingy hotel?'

'I'm not sure,' I said. 'I'm really not sure about any of this any more.'

Rob

114

* * *

I heard back from Jackie, Lewes's twinning chair, a few weeks after returning to London. She's the daughter of one of the boys who headed to Blois back in 1947. Here's what she told me:

'The link started in 1947 between two schoolmasters, one from Blois and the other from Lewes. Just after the end of World War II, M Robert Piolé, Senior English Master at the Lycée Augustin Thierry in Blois, conceived the idea that the boys of his school should visit England, perhaps on an exchange basis and, seeking a like-minded colleague in England, he wrote for assistance to the Cercle Francais in Brighton.

'The President, Mr Donald Moyes Auld, was Head of Modern Languages at Lewes County Grammar School for Boys, and, being a devoted Francophile, he replied immediately that he was interested.

'Thus it was on Monday, 17 March 1947 that a party of 67 boys led by Mr Auld left Lewes for Blois on the first school exchange. It lasted a week and was a huge success. My father was one of the school boys and he met a family in Blois who he has kept in contact with ever since. In fact they are like a second family to us – we have been to weddings and some of the family came to my wedding as well as sadly funerals.

'Lewes was officially twinned with Blois in 1963 when the civic charter was signed. Since then there have been many exchanges between all sorts of groups and lots of lovely friendships made. In 2013 we'll celebrate 50 years of twinning with a big get-together in Blois.

'Blois is a beautiful town and Lewes is very fortunate to be twinned with it.'

Hi Rob

I've always wanted to know more about Northampton and
its twin Poitiers in France. If you can find anything about it,
that would be something I didn't know. I'll leave it with you
to uncover what your journey wants you to.

Sam

15 · Poitiers
Twinned with Northampton

—

In which gangsters and scare stories appear

Dear Sam

Driving through Poitiers' central streets isn't something I'd advise. Although lined with terraces of attractive sand-coloured houses and courtyards of climbing plants, they're only just wide enough to carry a couple of shopping bags by your sides. Cars like KT with long noses don't really fit.

We now had a working satnav at least. Although we'd paid online for a map of western Europe, we hadn't been able to download it to my laptop and bung it on the satnav till Blois, where we'd found a good enough broadband connection. Stealing high-speed internet on the Continent wasn't easy, we'd discovered.

'This is the one,' I said to RG, as I squeezed into the world's smallest lift inside our hotel, like KT had squeezed into her parking space outside.

'The one what?' asked my girlfriend.

At the top of the lift I re-emerged. 'The town with the great twinning story. The town that gets me all enthusiastic again about twinning. We'll meet some important people here – I can feel it. First thing in the morning, I'm going straight to the town hall. Bam!'

'That's the spirit, my love,' said RG.

First thing the next morning, we headed to the greengrocers and bought bananas. Then, once we'd made our way through the maze of construction work that made Poitiers feel like Épinay-sur-Seine, I found a passage into *l'hotel de ville*.

RG followed me to the door. 'I'm going to get a coffee and do some writing.'

'Don't fancy coming in and hearing the best twinning story ever?'

She smiled. 'I'd rather have a coffee.'

We kissed goodbye and said we'd meet back at the café we'd spotted on Rue Lebascles. It'd looked all right from the outside – seats, lights, waiter. Nowhere to be overly concerned about leaving your other half.

Inside the town hall, I delivered my *jumelage* line like a pro. I even managed to ask for a *plan de la ville*. The little pinched-faced woman couldn't tell me anything about Northampton's relationship with Poitiers, but she knew a person who could. All I had to do was walk along Rue Victor Hugo and I'd come to the centre for Relations internationals et cooperation decentralise.

Away from the town hall, the roads of Poitiers were longer and wider. Quaint terraces became ugly offices and banks. The damp air of first thing had turned drier but a wind had picked up. It blew me around the corner of Rue Victor Hugo onto Rue Théophraste Renaudot, then onto Rue Aliénor d'Aquitaine, where eventually I found the gates to the international centre.

The site was Alcatraz. Behind the giant gates, three police cars were positioned like chess pieces. Around them stood stocky grey office blocks with streaks of dirty rain running like tears down their faces. A solitary tree, a prisoner, waved to me from the middle of the site.

I tried to stop a lady who'd just pumped a million numbers into the keypad beside the gate, but she was gone before I could ask any questions. I was James Bond, but locked away from the action.

After a few minutes of trying random combinations, a text came in from RG. 'Please come quickly. I don't feel safe.'

Like any good boyfriend, I set off straightaway. Like quite a bad boyfriend, I got a bit distracted by a side road that looked like it might lead to the Relations internationals et cooperation decentralise compound. With the feeling that RG could probably handle herself for another ten minutes, I walked through an unlocked gate at the end of Cité de la Traverse.

In a tiny box room inside a grey office filled with chatty middle-aged women sat a demure lady with a very big smile.

'Christiane Percevault?' I asked.

'Oui. Bonjour.'

The next 45 minutes disappeared in a warm chat with Christiane about 21st-century Poitiers and Europe. As I sat opposite her at her little desk, she tried to explain why her office was so well hidden. She shrugged her shoulders. '*Je ne sais pas*. I do not know.'

Poitiers, like Lorient, was struggling in its relationship with its English twin – largely because of a lack of enthusiasm from both sides, she told me. It wasn't not that nobody cared, but that not enough people cared enough.

Tucked away in a dismal grey compound outside the town centre, Christiane herself had no way of bringing attention to international relations – and she was the *chargée*. As she spoke, her voice was drowned out by diggers trying to redevelop her ageing town.

'It's so important,' said Christiane, sliding her hand through her silver hair. 'So important. We need to remember what happened during the wars. Town twinning does this. But we need more young people involved. Do you have any ideas how we can do this?'

'A third world war?' I joked.

Christiane smiled. 'You need to be careful, especially in England. If you do not get involved with Europe, Rob, it could be bad for international relationships. You cannot keep by yourself. You need to cross the water and visit us – like *you* are doing.'

My phone chimed in my pocket.

'Christiane, I'm sorry, I have to go. I need to rescue someone.'

'Is everything ok?' she asked.

'I hope so,' I replied, taking her hand like it was a dear friend's.

My new confidant walked me back to the gate and we European-kissed good-bye. 'Please come back,' she said as I strode away. 'Come back and say hello again.' I promised I would.

Back at the café, RG was just finishing up.

'What's wrong?' I asked.

She looked to her left, then to her right. 'It's the mafia,' she whispered.

'What's the mafia?'

'Sssshhhh,' she insisted. 'Everyone, everywhere. We need to leave.'

Inside the tourist information centre in the beautiful old part of town, RG refused to tell me what had happened in the café. Instead she went off to take photos of the 11th-century church of Notre-Dame-la-Grande and some doors. I popped into a bookshop to pick up a couple of road maps – to further ease the rest of our journeys around the Continent.

I got chatting to the big-faced man behind the counter and managed, in French, to explain that I was touring Europe. He beamed and began rooting around under his counter.

'Go, visit, see, you must go here,' he said, handing me a red tourist's guide covered in gold stars. 'It is the best to visit for you.'

'China?' I asked. 'But I'm touring Europe.'

'Go there. It is the future.'

Back at the church, RG wasn't convinced by China. She favoured Spain, which, I agreed, made more sense as we had to cross it to get to our next twin, Porto. Plus it was about 4,000 miles closer than China.

A coffee and tea in a tiny café near where RG had nearly run over a tipsy Frenchman the night before completed our time in Poitiers. The roads around us were beautiful and, we'd decided after spending over a fortnight in France, very French. And we, sitting back, thanking in *mercis, bonne journée-ing* and *excusez-moi-ing*, had become a couple of Francophiles.

After two weeks' travelling through the country, from Douai to Paris, across to Normandy and Brittany, then south through Château-Gontier, Blois and now Poitiers, we'd started to feel very comfortable in France.

'I've been thinking,' I said to RG, tucking into a biscuit. 'After that chat with lovely Christiane, I just wonder where town twinning's going. It clearly has a big, hugely important history. But it seems there's no future. Not because nobody cares, just because there's so much else going on these days.

'It's now easy to go to France on holiday – you don't need to stay with a family, though of course that adds something. All those things that made town twinning so important in the 50s and 60s seem to have faded away.'

'It's a shame,' said RG. 'We've met such lovely people and learnt so much about everywhere we've been.'

'It's scary,' I said. 'I mean what if town twinning doesn't have a role any more?'

Rob

Hi Rob,

What a fantastic idea!

I recall learning that Porto, Portugal, is Bristol's twin
town. I'd love to visit Porto for the wine, architecture and
Old World vibe: apparently, chickens still stroll through
certain neighbourhoods, the sort where old men play
board games outdoors.

I look forward to hearing more about your adventures.

Take care,
Doe

16 · Porto
Twinned with Bristol

—

In which a woman called Rachel refuses to crack

Dear Doe

I could tell you a billion things about Porto's approach to international relations. I could wax lyrical about operational axes, tell you story after story of predefined visions and missions. Oh how you'd laugh at tales of operational tools and diplomatic and consular representations.

Inside Porto's town hall, we heard about all this from a girl called Rachel. She'd told the angry man downstairs that she was expecting us (she wasn't). And she was very keen to share some information.

From the moment RG and I sat at Rachel's desk, I'd got the sense Porto wouldn't be the place for twin town nuggets. In fact, from the moment I'd driven KT into an underground car park and reversed tentatively back up because she couldn't clear the bottom of the ramp, I'd had a bad feeling about Porto. Saying that, I was probably too high on burning clutch fumes to make any big judgements.

We'd only parked in Garagem Batalha because the car park of the B&B Hotel we should have parked in was so rammed with cars, vans and bikes that the only way to leave was to bash the vehicle in front of you to one side. After watching a demonstration of this by a flustered Portuguese lady, I decided KT would be happier elsewhere.

All we knew about Porto before our visit was that it had a lot of port, the moreish fortified wine, inside its walls. But then so did Tesco. My goal for our visit to your twin was to increase my knowledge of Porto tenfold – so I had more Porto stories than Tesco stories. Plus I wanted some idea of why this coastal city that always looked so old-worldly in photos was twinned with Bristol, which, I'd learnt from my three visits there, was always a bit grey and wet.

We found our way to Ponte Luis I. It was evening time. Across the sparkling Douro, giant placards of local port producers were lit before the setting sun. There was Cálem, Graham's, Taylor's and a few more illegible signs further along the river.

'Tomorrow,' said RG with a wicked smile on her face, 'let's taste some port.'

'For breakfast?' I asked.

'Yeah. Why not? Then ice cream for dinner.'

'Really?' I asked.

'Course not, silly.'

We woke the next morning in the B&B Hotel – a slightly charmless but very neat and comfortable chain of hotels where the second B, the breakfast, was never included – and headed to the river to find the Romantic museum and port museum. It was May 1st, Labour Day to the Portuguese. A day to celebrate the achievements of the workers in the country. And how did they celebrate this hard work? They closed all the museums and galleries and took the day off.

'Closed,' said RG, as we reached Vinho do Porto.

We walked back to the centre of the city up Rua Tomás Gonzaga and Rua de S João Novo. The roads were grim – lined with derelict, windowless houses that I'm sure once were stunning. If we'd seen an old man and chicken, I imagine they would've been trying to mug each other. RG was convinced she'd spotted a crack den at one point, as she peeked through a hole in a fence. We tweeted it.

Our good friend Miles from Bristol replied: 'Sounds like Bristol!'

The rest of our day disappeared buying coats in shops that weren't observing Labour Day, consuming cakes and rip-off tea in tourist cafés, and slopping through the streets, as rain once again drizzled into our faces. RG, I was learning, really wasn't a rain or cold person. Long walks through wet city streets often turned into solo missions, as she hung back or sheltered in shoe shops.

By the time evening had arrived, my heels hurt, my back ached and my thighs were burning. But at least the rain had cleared for the evening, leaving just swipes of charcoal cloud above Ponte Luis I.

'Leave this to me,' I said to RG, closing in on a restaurant by the river.

'English?' asked a tall, thin, open-collared waiter.

'Um. Yes,' I replied.

'Then we are the perfect restaurant for you. What you want, boss and lady?'

I turned to RG and smiled.

'Just looking,' I said.

He nodded his head and stepped back.

I turned to RG and whispered, 'That wasn't supposed to happen.'

'What wasn't?' she asked.

'He was supposed to offer us a free bottle of wine. That's what they do on Lygon Street in Melbourne. Or money off a poppadum, like in Brick Lane.'

RG smiled at the waiter, then looked back to me. 'Shall we try another one?'

We tried the same trick at every café and restaurant we could find. Not one waiter offered us a free anything.

RG looked me bang in the eyes, smiled and held my hand. 'You're a bit of an idiot sometimes. You know that?'

Francesinha, a sloppy Portuguese version of a croque monsieur, with wine took place in either Peter, a restaurant with a whale above the entrance, or Restaurante Mercearia. I don't remember. I do remember, however, that the bottle of wine had a lovely name and an even lovelier taste. I spent the last part of the meal joining in a conversation between a Dutch couple and the owner of the restaurant on a subject I knew nothing about. I don't remember my contribution but I'd guess it was witty.

Then we went port tasting.

In Vinologia, a tall woman-shaped blur sat us near the door and offered us lots of different port options. After hearing us mumble something, she disappeared before returning with six glasses, three each, and three bottles of port. She proceeded to pour the port into the glasses.

I did most of the talking that night. I think I compared one port to a chocolatey coffee and then went on to explain that I prefered tea to coffee. RG would have been very embarrassed, I'm sure, had she not been trying to keep her food and drink inside her body. With the port came RG's favourite part of the evening: the cherry chocolate cake with chocolate sauce. I'd never seen a pair of inebriated eyes light up so quickly and so brightly.

Even the next morning, as we dragged our hungover bodies towards the town hall, RG was praising the previous night's dessert.

'We had *dessert* last night?' I teased.

Rachel in the city hall was lovely really. Suited and made-up, she sat opposite me and RG with a perma-grin, flanked either side by two more ladies tapping fiercely at computers. For half an hour she told us all those technical things about international relations I listed earlier.

We asked why Porto and Bristol would twin in the first place.

'It is an interesting fact that there is a port history between Porto and Bristol. Between Porto and Great Britain more. There is the port makers like Taylor's and Graham's – they are families that have come from Britain and made businesses here. It is rather important this wine interest.

'And it is rather important that Marmaduke Alderson was Lord Mayor of Bristol and then was chairman of the Bristol International Twinning Association for 18 years. Mr Alderson did a lot for the twinning, including making the Foundation, which is rather important.'

Rachel went on to tell us that since 2000 the relationship had become 'not so active'. However, the Bristol Oporto Association's website suggested otherwise. In 2012, at the time of our visit, Marmaduke Alderson's Foundation was still going strong. One recently funded event was Portugal Day – a time for the children of a school in Bristol to celebrate all things Portuguese. Infants and juniors got stuck into dance, music, art and language activities. The smiles on the faces of the kids involved revealed what a huge success it was.

Our new twinning connection listed fact after fact about Porto's approach to international relationships. We squeezed a few human stories out of her – that people from the twinning association had weekly meetings and went to dinner parties, that you have to be an active member of the Bristol or Porto community to become a member – but she was holding back. Her answers were too polished, her smile too practised. Until I asked one final question.

'Would you like to go to Bristol?'

She put down her copy of 'PORTO CITY COUNCIL – International Relations Reference Framework' and looked at me.

'I would very much like to visit Bristol and hope to make my visit next year.'

Rob

Hi Rob

How about Cordoba? In Andalusia. Twinned with
my hometown Manchester. Apparently 'The origins
of Cordoba are lost in the mists of time'. Sounds cool
to me. Will you find out what it means for me?

Owen

17 · Cordoba
Twinned with Manchester

—

In which the rain in Spain falls mainly

Dear Owen

'Lisbon here we come,' said RG, as we pulled out of Garagem Batalha in Porto.

'Cordoba,' I corrected. 'In Spain. Lisbon's in Portugal. We're going to Spain now.'

'You really are silly sometimes,' said RG. 'Remember Ana?'

My girlfriend reminded me that we weren't heading to your twin yet. Instead, we were spending a couple of nights just south of Lisbon in a place called Cascais. I'd arranged it one tipsy evening in London. Our friend Ana had told us we were welcome to stay with her parents if we were heading to Portugal. I'd slurred a big yes please, apparently.

That first night in Cascais, we went ballroom dancing.

I'd be lying if I said I was a good dancer. At school, during dance class, I was always the last to be picked. Once, the final girl to choose a partner tried to explain to the teacher she'd learn more from dancing by herself.

Over the years, beer has become my ideal dancing companion. But that night in Cascais – a pretty coastal town made of wrinkled long-timers and blistered Brits abroad – there was no bar. It was me, RG, Ana's parents and a handful of locals who'd been polishing their ballroom skills for years.

'You did well, Rob,' said Ana's Spanish mum over dinner the next day.

RG beamed. 'You were brilliant. After you loosened up. And when your hips started to move. Once the old man teacher had put his hand on your thigh.'

We laughed.

'Well. Done. Rob.' Geoffrey poured me a little more wine. Then he turned to RG. 'But you. What a natural. What a *great* dancer.'

The next morning, RG drove us away from warm, sunny Portugal back into Spain, where only days before I'd driven us through snowy mountains.

'What do you think these signs mean?' she asked, still dancing but this time to Beyoncé.

'They're another road charge. Like the tolls but more tax-y. Apparently the Portuguese government's taxing everything these days. A sign that Europe's trying to shut people out?'

We could see the border crossing creeping nearer.

RG looked to me, mid-Beyoncé pose. 'Hey, we're in Spain now anyway. *Hola!*'

During our two days in Cascais, when we weren't strolling the coast or being squeezed by old men in dance lessons, I was looking into the relationship between Cordoba and Manchester. Everyone we'd spoken to before leaving the UK had questioned it, like it was never meant to be or like it was doomed to failure. Other than terribly unreliable Wikipedia, no website gave us anything.

While RG focused on keeping us on the road, I took in the views across the Andalusian hills. The walls of green. The dripping leaves. The thick woods around every corner. The lanes wandering away from the main roads. The lumps, bumps and undulations.

We arrived outside your twin a couple of hours later. It was a 20-minute walk to the city walls from our hotel, through a park, around giant puddles, along a river and across the beautiful, wide, sandy-coloured Roman bridge.

'If it doesn't work, what are we going to do?' I asked RG, as we crossed the bridge.

'What do you mean?'

'Town twinning,' I said. 'Surely there's some way we can help make it big again. Maybe I can get chatting to councils back home – get them to pull their fingers out.'

'They're half the problem, aren't they?' said RG. 'They can do stuff now, already, without us. Massive stuff. But they're not.'

'That's why perhaps I should,' I said.

The forecast for the next day was a mix of heavy rain and light rain with a chance of occasional seriously heavy rain. So we gave ourselves a brief tour of the city before bed. Within seconds, we'd reached the towering walls of a giant mosque.

'This is it,' said RG. 'This is the place Ana's mum said about.'

Nearby, a portly Spanish man was caressing a classical guitar beside a pretty, olive-skinned lady. She was wailing skywards like a wolf.

'It's probably her dress,' I whispered to RG. 'Too tight.'

RG tutted. 'She's beautiful.'

Cordoba, we learnt back at the hotel, was founded by the Romans. It was a hugely important strategic position for them, at the highest navigable point of the Guadalquivir River. They used the waterway, which opened to the sea at

Sanlúcar de Barrameda, to ship olive oil and wine back home.

As we woke to more Andalusian showers the following morning, home was exactly where I wanted to be.

'*Paraguas, sombrilla, paraguas,*' shouted a man from the back of a white transit near the bridge. 'Keep you dry. *Paraguas*. Keep you dry, British.'

Through the city gates we sheltered under the canopy of one of the many gift shops. A thousand *paraguas* followed us across the bridge. Umbrellas of every colour, decorated in every flag. Underneath each was a confused holidaymaker – like us, wondering why Brittany's weather had come to southern Spain.

'Let's do the Mezquita,' said RG, smiling inside her hood.

'Mez-key-wah?'

'The thing with the big walls we saw last night. It's a mosque – it was one of the biggest in Islam. Didn't you listen to Ana's mum?'

'Was it when I was dancing?' I asked. 'I have to concentrate hard when I'm dancing. Moves like those don't just happen.'

The Mezquita was the great mosque of Cordoba. Work started on it in 785, a little over half a century after the Moors had conquered the city. The Moors crossed to the Iberian peninsula from Algeria and Morocco in the early 8th century and, after bringing most of Iberia under Islamic rule, set up an emirate in Cordoba.

In 1236, the Christians took Cordoba back. But they were so blown away by the beauty of the Mezquita, they left it standing – building a cathedral between its arches and columns.

There were fewer umbrellas outside now, which made our journey to the

Mezquita quick and painless. But as soon as we walked through the gateway into the columned courtyard, we discovered why. Everyone had descended on the mosque.

Instead of joining two non-moving queues, we bought a musical potato from a tall man with sunken eyes. Within seconds, RG was jamming with him.

Lacking an instrument, I wandered off into the tourist information office. But learnt nothing. A sun-kissed lady told me my best bet was the international office in the town hall across the city.

'Great. Where is that?' I asked.

'Today?' she said. 'It's closed.'

'Bloody buggering hell,' I may have responded.

If we wanted to spend time in Cordoba and couldn't get into the Mezquita, we should lose ourselves in the alleyways, patios and courtyards, she suggested.

Tropical gardens, art installations, towering palm trees, family gatherings, exhibitions full of mirrors, condom and sex-toy dispensers: you name it, we found it in the courtyards of Cordoba.

RG headed into an exhibition while I peered through railings at lime and orange trees, speckled with raindrops. A minute later, she reappeared beyond the gate and handed me an orange. The moment – the beautiful girl emerging into a garden of fruit – was perfectly, Biblically dreamy. Then I popped a furry, soggy, warm, deflated piece of bitter orange into my mouth and choked.

The streets of the city centre opened up beyond the courtyards. Near the very closed town hall, we discovered Roman ruins. Hanging close-by were flags promoting 'CORDOBA 2016 – Ciudad Europea de la Cultura' and 'OFICIANA

CAPITALIDAD CULTURAL'.

'Isn't Manchester trying to be the European capital of culture or something?' I asked.

'Maybe that's the connection,' said RG. 'It's a competitive connection – they're both trying to beat each other.'

'Or was that Liverpool?' I asked. 'A few years ago?'

This was getting too much. Not uncovering anything juicy about these twins was weighing heavy. My heels were starting to drag with every failure to find a fascinating titbit. It was the guilt – the feeling that someone back home was waiting for an answer I just couldn't find.

As we splashed back through the tiny, pretty streets and picked up a postcard that again, like in Benodet, looked nothing like the sodden scene before us, I went online on my phone. It was bad news.

RG stepped out of a shop to see my head hanging.

'What's wrong?' she asked. 'You look sad.'

'I don't know how to break this to you,' I said, not able to look her in the eyes.

'What?' she asked.

I wiped a raindrop from her cheek. 'We've lost a twin.'

Rob

Hi Rob,

Apparently Monmouth is twinned with Carbonne in
the south-west of France. I've only just found out about
it so I know nothing more. I wasn't really curious until
I found your website.

It sounds like a bonkers trip, and also totally fascinating.

Good luck!

Anita

18 · Carbonne
Twinned with Monmouth

—

In which many hurdles are overcome

Dear Anita

Cordoba and Manchester weren't twins. They were friends.

As I read Manchester's council website outside the tourist shop near the Mezquita in Cordoba, I realised this wasn't great for our twin town adventure. Manchester's main twin, it seemed, was Chemnitz in Germany. Things were going from bad to really, really rubbish.

'Lucky we're doing Chemnitz too, then,' said RG, finding the positive.

Travelling this closely with my girlfriend had started to reveal a lot. We'd learnt you have to compromise all the time, every day. When I wanted to nip into another tourist office and RG didn't, she had to be ok with that. When she wanted time alone, I had to leave her be. We also had to sweep squabbles under the car mat and put them down to living in each other's pocket.

Comfort was a thing of the past. Stress was a constant. Almost every day we had to look up places to stay or wander into guesthouses and hotels and ask for a room in a language we couldn't speak. It didn't matter how hungry, sleepy or stressed we felt, we had to do it.

KT now had a slow puncture, which meant long journeys were being chopped up and turned frustrating. And her engine kept burning petrol, meaning we needed to put more in all the time. Then there were the dingy B&Bs, navigational mishaps and our disappearing budget.

But it was the weather that was hammering us. Every day it rained. Not only was KT's hood starting to leak, our waterproofs were taking in water too. Everything had dampened: our jumpers and trousers and jeans and shoes and socks and, although we weren't yet saying it to each other, our spirits.

We left Cordoba drenched and drove south east towards Almeria, where we'd arranged to take a short break with our friend Alex.

One evening, after RG had gone to bed, Alex and I watched the full moon rise over nearby Mojacar. With a fair bit of wine and port in me, while sitting below my other old friend the moon, I emptied all my feelings.

'Sounds like you're doing all right, mate,' Alex said, drinking some port and eating a pork-flavoured corn nut. 'You've done a shitload and you haven't killed each other yet. That's cool.'

The next day, the sun revealed itself and the temperature soared. We drove from the villa towards the Pyrenees with top down, sunglasses on, backs stuck to seats and our hands touching on the gear stick. I'm not sure exactly what had happened, but everything felt a little easier.

We carved our way up and down the mountains. We stood and posed before sweeping panoramas. In Oliana, a town that was just a street on a hill dwarfed by yet more mountains, we picnicked in late spring sunshine and watched soft shadows steal our view. The day we reached Carbonne, your twin, we glided over tight, rocky lanes and around jutting cliffs and meandered along roads we felt would never end.

We were back on track, snapping photos from the top of the car, joking about our inability to speak other languages, and playing Guess The Price of Petrol on the one road through Andorra. As we parked up in baking sunshine and ordered a couple of beers outside a little café in your pretty French twin, the omens were good.

Carbonne was more than just pretty. At the top of a hill just outside the town centre, we could still see the picket-fence Pyrenees on the horizon. In the *centre ville* itself, two shopping streets – this evening tinted by sunshine – ran parallel and ended near a bridge.

'Pont de Jumelage,' shouted RG, pointing to the sign beside the bridge.

We had a lot of beer inside us now.

'Woo,' I shouted in response, my shorts rippling in the warm wind.

We took about a thousand photos of the sign, me posing differently in each.

'Do we have time to go to the tourist office?' I shouted again.

'Oui! You go. I'll find a Carrefour and get us some food.'

I wobbled along Rue Gambetta towards Place de la Republique, where I tried to have a chat with a man in the tourist info. Lucky for us both I became fluent in French after three beers. Or my sign language for 'book about the area' was spot on.

At a bench overlooking a still river, I skimmed through 'Great Tourist Sites in Midi-Pyrenees'. Every flick of a page revealed more wonder. The cathedral of Saint-Bertrand-de-Comminges bursting from luscious green hills at the foot of the mountains. The limestone circles of Cirque de Gavarnie. Jazz in Gers. The 'majestic Canal des Deux Mers'.

RG reappeared and sat beside me.

'I want to move to the south of France,' I told her.

'You wanted to move to Lorient a week ago,' she replied.

'And now I want to move to the Pyrenees, please.' I yawned a tipsy-tired yawn.

RG dumped a bag of snacks on the ground. 'The supermarket was miles and miles and miles away,' she said.

And then I fell asleep on her lap.

The next morning, I found myself queuing at the town hall. But this time it was different. I had no expectations and very little hope of a story. It'd become a sort of habit by now, like brushing my teeth before bed.

I reached the desk and asked the sniffling lady if she spoke English.

'Oui. Yes. I do. How can I help?'

Carole's excellent grasp of English had come from three years of living in Boston, America, and some time spent in England and Ireland. She told me about adventures similar to mine, jumping between countries, meeting new people, experiencing the unexpected everywhere she travelled.

'But never anything *that* big,' she said, holding in a sneeze. 'You are both good and brave. And you are lucky to travel so much. It is the best thing to do to improve your life.'

After calling nine locals and holding up the queue trying to help me, Carole uncovered the story of how her town had come to be twinned with yours.

It started in the early 1970s when a young man called Jean-Pierre decided to become an English teacher. He travelled to Wales as part of his studies and visited Monmouth. He fell for the town. When he returned to France, he tried to find a way to connect Carbonne and Monmouth, to keep a friendship going. The answer was rugby. Soon, Carbonne's rugby boys were rolling around on a Welsh field with Monmouth's.

In 1975, both towns signed the official charter. 'And I think the relationship is still strong today,' sniffled Carole.

Limbering up for the junior hurdles down by the assault course we'd found the day before, I turned to RG. 'It's about the people and the places,' I said. 'It's about people like Jean-Pierre visiting Monmouth and making friends. And people like us coming here and meeting people like Carole and jumping hurdles like these. We are good and brave.'

'I'm not sure this is what she meant by that comment,' said RG.

But I was off before she could argue her point. I flung my legs as high as I could over the first hurdle and followed that with what can only be described as a graceful descent the other side. Each of the following obstacles was defeated by a mix of poise and flair. My brain played me the 'Chariots of Fire' theme as each jump felt like another town twinning hurdle overcome.

As we crossed back into Carbonne via the twin town bridge, RG showed me footage of a gangly fool tumbling over ten hurdles on her phone.

'What a knob,' I said, chuckling. 'You've Been Framed?'

RG kept replaying it and laughing. 'Watch your legs. It's like when you dance – all weird and unnatural.'

We bounced back along La Garonne, waving to Carole, who'd popped outside the Mairie for a sneeze. Then we slid into KT, got her purring and headed on towards Clermont l'Herault, again with nowhere to stay but now with more hope in our hearts.

The pressure, for the first time in four weeks, felt like it had dropped.

Rob

Rob

There's a rather dull industrial suburb of north Bristol, which borders Filton Airfield and is home to a large Rolls Royce factory, called Patchway. It's twinned with a lovely little town in the south of France, known for its wine and olive oil, called Clermont l'Herault. I used to holiday near here as a child.

I can see no earthly reason why the two are twinned...

Miles

19 · Clermont l'Herault Twinned with Patchway

—

In which there is a difficult conversation

Dear Miles

What a difference a week makes. From snow in northern Spain to yet more sweatingly-scorchy sunshine in the south of France.

'Bit hot for me,' I said to RG, driving us over a mountainous speed bump at one end of Clermont l'Herault's main street. 'Look out for hotel signs. I'm not really concentrating any more. Too hot.'

On our third pass of the town, we still couldn't spot a hotel. So we decided to follow signs to Lake Salagou instead, a big blue blob on our huge roadmap of France.

The roads narrowed outside town. There were fewer people and fewer cars. Our satnav now displayed just a thin, curving white line on a lime green background. But we sensed the lake and the sun was setting and the leaves were letting streaks of daffodil yellow through and onto KT's bonnet. We spoke about how beautiful a sunset would look over a big blue blob so we went on, over rickety bridges and along tracks barely wide enough for us.

'Oh my,' said RG, as we curved our way through a tiny, stony village called something like Liaison. 'Look.'

It appeared from nowhere – calm and glimmering in the bosom of stubbled hills and mounds of red soil. Not a word passed between us as we sat and looked out to the lake. No battered Citroëns chugged, no planes left vapour trails overhead, not even a bird dared whisper. As the sun dropped behind the hills, RG and I glanced at each other with movie smiles.

Clermont l'Herault was a market town where very good-looking French people clearly spent much of their time in the sunshine. Everywhere we looked we saw olive groves and vineyards.

As evening arrived, we sat in the only restaurant quiet enough to take us and chose dinner like pros. French food, we decided, was delicious. And with the ability to order *une carafe d'eau*, understand *cru* and *à point*, and order another beer with a nonchalant *encore s'il vous plait*, the whole French dining experience had become rather tasty and relaxing.

'I'm going to miss France,' said RG, as we got *l'addition*.

'*Moi aussi*,' I replied.

That night, we wandered the streets, looking out for a twinning sign.

'Miles said Patchway's near Bristol and it's dull and industrial. So we need to find something dull and industrial here in stunning Clermont l'Herault,' I said to RG.

'Like the olive trees and glorious wine?' she asked.

'Yeah, just like that.'

'And the big, massive beautiful lake?' she continued.

'Precisely.'

We found nothing even remotely dull and industrial about your twin except a petrol station. But even that had pretty trees around it.

'This place is too lovely,' I said to RG. 'It's like Eden but nicer. Let's just enjoy its best bits.'

'What are you planning, my dear?' asked RG.

'Tomorrow morning. 5am. Let's watch us some sunrise over the big blue blob.'

RG smiled. 'Yes. Love it. Let's.'

Five in the morning, it turned out, was a painful hour. Also, as lovely a target as it was, it was actually impossible to get out of bed then. A sleepy RG nudged me to tell me the birds outside the window were 'going nuts'. We, however, were drifting back to dreams of mountain drives and sunset-lit lakes.

The sun had started to light the night's clouds as we parked in Liaison at around 6.30am. At the edge of the lake, caravans were already glowing. A tiny black Labrador-cross trotted up, rubbed itself against me, then wandered on to dip its paws in the still water.

At that moment – as the sun crept higher behind the pillow clouds, a puppy played at the edge of a stunning lake, and my girlfriend took a million photos – everything felt right with the world again. As the minutes passed, men in 4x4s towing dinghies and fishing boats crunched over the gravel. They boomed *bonjours* to one another before gliding towards the horizon.

Back in town later that morning, we sat on a bench for a breakfast of shop-bought cereal from bathroom-washed shop-bought coleslaw tubs with tricky-to-track-down-supermarket milk splashed on top.

'How are you doing?' I asked RG, slurping some milky muesli.

'Yeah, fine. I think,' she replied, watching three young French boys whacking a football into old couples ambling past in the warm sunshine.

'Sure?' I asked, taking a final slurp of milk.

'Rob, honest. I'm enjoying myself.'

'Really?' I asked.

She sighed. 'It's tough at times, yes. And we're always doing stuff together, which is fine. Difficult, sometimes, I guess. But we knew that was going to happen. Right?'

'And?' I asked.

'Maybe, just maybe, possibly, we should spend a bit of time apart.'

'You want to go home,' I concluded. 'I knew it.'

'No, silly. Just some time apart. When we get to Avignon. Just so we're not too... in each other's pockets. Just half a day or something. I need to know I can still walk down a street by myself.'

'Of course you can. I don't mind. I'll let you.'

RG sighed. 'That's exactly what I mean.'

That afternoon, walking alongside RG to *l'office de tourisme*, the last place I wanted to be was by my girlfriend's side. I felt I'd clipped her wings, stopped her exploring in her own way and stifled her.

At the tourist office, Sabine had just closed the door before we walked in.

'*Fermé?*' we asked. '*Anglais? S'il vous plait.*'

We asked the usual questions – why Clermont l'Herault and Patchway, what happens between the two, when did it start, what's happened since? Sabine answered each question with a shrug and an 'I'm sorry, I don't know'.

'Nobody knows anything about town twinning. It's ridiculous,' I said, in a moment of frustration that took me back to being in Waltham Abbey and not finding the answers I wanted that misty January morning when this had all begun.

'Though I met my husband because of town twinning,' said Sabine, fetching a couple of leaflets from behind her desk.

'You...' I started then ran out of words.

'My husband and I met when I was 15 years of age and visiting my twin town.'

'Please tell us more,' implored RG.

German Sabine was living in her homeland at the time. Her husband-to-be, just a friend when they were teenagers and exploring life through international exchange programmes, was from a small town in France. They met, they got along, they stayed in touch, they met again and they married.

'So town twinning is very important to me and my husband,' said Sabine. 'Without it we would never have met and fallen in love.'

Before long, Sabine had found Patchway Twinning Association's website, which revealed a little of the relationship's history. But I wanted to know more because, like you, I could see no earthly reason why the two were twinned.

'You have a car?' asked Sabine.

'Indeed.'

'Then you must see the lake of Salagou.'

'We've been there. Twice,' said RG. 'It's beautiful.'

Sabine picked up a leaflet she'd left for us on the desk. 'Then you must see this instead. It is the most lovely place. And driving it is the most beautiful drive.'

Rob

* * *

After the trip, John Thomas, chairman of the twinning association, told me Patchway and Clermont l'Herault twinned in 1995, soon after Patchway had been promoted from parish to town status. The town wanted to celebrate this and find new friends by starting a relationship with somewhere near Hanover, Germany, which was already twinned with big brother Bristol. But that was a non-starter. All the towns near Bristol had already snaffled Hanover's twins.

This left Patchway with a dilemma: forget the twinning idea and focus on developing as a town, or look outside Hanover, or even outside Germany. Back then, John was 'on the periphery' of the twinning association. He watched from middle distance as the new organisation went to CORTA meetings and eventually got in touch with the little picturesque French town of Clermont l'Herault, near where you holidayed as a boy. (CORTA was a regional forum set up to help towns around Bristol and Cheltenham twin. It doesn't exist any more.)

John remembers the early visits and exchanges vividly. Mainly because of the 23-hour coach journey through England and France. Today he can fly it in two hours. The relationship, he told me, is very strong. The Patchway group is like family to the French – they're even close enough to get stuck into each other's town gossip.

Hi Rob

I grew up in Colchester which is twinned with Wetzlar in Germany, Avignon in France and Imola in Italy. I'd recommend Avignon so you can go Sur le pont d'Avignon like in that song.

Thanks, Emma

20 · Avignon
Twinned with Colchester
—

In which Rob must try to avoid temptation

Dear Emma

RG needed time alone. She hadn't just suggested it with her body language, now she'd said it with real words. And I knew, because of the unspoken rules we'd created for the trip, I had to give it to her. But how?

We'd taken Sabine's advice and stopped off in Saint-Guilhem-le-Désert, an interlinking joy of cobbled streets and courtyard cafés and restaurants below a rocky retreat that, it turned out, was the ruin of a castle. This beautiful *bastide*, a fortified town, was also a place for pilgrims to stop off on their way to Santiago de Compostela in Spain.

After a couple of hours of exploring, together, hand in hand, we headed for Avignon, where again we had nowhere to sleep. But that wasn't so stressful any more. Not in France. We'd got used to booking rooms last minute, at the doorstep of the hotel, in a form of French.

Like you and everyone else in the world, Avignon had meant one thing to me before our visit. Dancing on a bridge. Because, as the old French ditty goes,

> *Sur le pont d'Avignon*
> *L'on y danse, l'on y danse*
> *Sur le pont d'Avignon*
> *L'on y danse tous en rond*

Driving into the heart of the city – just as we'd tried to avoid – I looked out for le pont d'Avignon. Top down in KT, this should have been easy. But, unless we were on it, the famous bridge was hiding. We drove around the confusing one-way system twice before I pleaded with RG not to let me take the wrong road again. But my words were lost in the gales that surrounded us. So we went around the confusing one-way system once more, keeping our eyes peeled for a cheap-looking hotel.

A month in, money was now an issue. The question was no longer, *Can we spend another ten euros on a hotel room?* It was, *Have we got ten euros for dinner?* Some accidental splashing out on haute cuisine had left us with half our budget remaining and well over half our journey to go. And KT, safe in the gated car park of the hotel, was running up her own unseen costs – parking fees, road tolls and taxes, oil top-ups. From baguettes to bedrooms, everything was starting to feel pricier than before.

The next morning in Avignon, when RG told me we should head back to Carrefour, France's answer to Tesco, for some reason I didn't react well. I thought about some advice my dad had once given me to 'never go back'. Taking it completely literally, I refused to turn around. I tried to explain that going back was a big mistake with arguments like, 'Nah, I don't want to. Let's find the bridge.' But my girlfriend's reasoning was sound. We had no food and because it was Sunday supermarkets would soon close. No turning back meant no budget lunch.

With a huff, RG stomped off to the supermarket. With a sigh, I wandered towards the river to find the bridge.

Most people know the bridge that crosses the Rhone in Avignon as the pont d'Avignon. But if you're a local you probably call it Pont Saint-Bénézet, after the shepherd boy who was convinced he'd been ordered by angels to build a river crossing here. The legend goes that Bénézet ('Little Benedict') was having an ordinary day in the Vivarias region of south-east France when a voice told him to build the bridge. The impressionable type, Bénézet headed straight for Avignon to tell people what he had to do.

Little Benedict's big task didn't excite the people of the town as much as he'd hoped. To stop their scoffing, he decided to prove his faith by lifting a big stone and carrying it into the Rhone. It worked. Several locals were blown away by his determination and superhuman strength and leapt in after him to start work.

It's difficult to say how much truth there is in the Little Benedict story. But Bénézet was definitely a real man and was definitely interred on the bridge after his death in 1184.

Looking out at the bridge from an archway I'd reached by following an excitable bunch of Japanese tourists, I questioned why Bénézet had only built half of it. I looked around for an explanation but instead got whacked in the face by a cardboard box.

The gales were strengthening. Japanese tourists were now floating across the sky in front of me. With no sign of RG, I headed up an old stone staircase and back to the *centre ville* to find the Palais de Papes, a building featured in our tourist guides from Carbonne.

In the next half hour, I'd done Avignon. I'd meandered lonely and inelegantly as a wind-buffeted cloud, taking in views of the river from a pretty garden between the bridge and the palace, admiring the façade of the Palais de Papes, and watching groups of French youths sing sweetly around a guitar.

'*Bonjour, monsieur. Habitez-vous à Avignon?*' asked two pretty girls.

'*Non, pardon,*' I said. '*Je suis Anglais.*'

They smiled. 'Our English is not good, monsieur. But we thought you would be a man we should talk to.'

I looked around for RG, suspicious she might have set this up. If she hadn't then while she was buying me lunch, probably quite upset and definitely very hungry, I was being hit on by two French girls.

I froze for a second, then smiled. 'Your English is very good,' I said.

The girls looked to each other and giggled.

'Monsieur,' said the shorter, frizzier-haired one, 'we have a question for you.'

'We hope it is not rude to ask,' said the other.

I blinked hard then smiled. 'Oui?'

The wild-haired French girl reached out her hand and touched my arm. Her friend, looking deep into my eyes and smiling, did the same.

'Monsieur,' they said together, 'God loves you and wants you to visit his concert. Will you join him of the afternoon?'

'Um...'

I didn't join God of the afternoon. Instead, I hurried back to the bridge – helped a little by the wind – to track down my girlfriend. My mood had mellowed since our tiff. Being side by side with RG was, I'd decided on my walk back past the town square through millions of shutter-happy tourists, better than exploring towns alone.

I spotted her by Pont Saint-Bénézet, her dark hair swept across her face, her hands rooted in her multi-coloured raincoat pockets, and her sorry-looking baguette broken in two. We hugged and apologised.

'How do you get on it?' shouted RG, toppling back and looking up.

'You can't, it seems,' I shouted back.

'*They* have,' shouted RG, pointing to the hundreds of tourists wobbling up and down the half-bridge.

'They were the lucky ones.'

RG smiled. 'How about "*Sous le pont d'Avignon*"? Just as good, innit.'

I learnt the old French ditty started life as something closer to 'Sous le pont d'Avignon', like RG had joked. It was *under* the bridge people would have enjoyed drinks in the cafés and danced into the night. Dancing *sur* le pont would have been dangerous as the bridge was too narrow.

Many original arches that had once taken Pont Saint-Bénézet across the Rhone to Villeneuve-lès-Avignon on the opposite bank crumbled after 1185. When the bridge opened, dancers would have ronde'd under 22 stone arches. When we visited, just four arches remained. This was largely the fault of the 1668 flood, which swept much of Little Benedict's bridge downstream.

We lunched on broken baguette, ham and cheese back in the windy gardens, while boy scouts somersaulted ahead of us. I told RG it was a good thing we'd bought lunch early, as I'd suggested, as the shops would be closed by now. She tossed her eyes and we laughed.

As hard as we searched, together, hand in hand, for signs of Colchester, we found nothing. With time disappearing and a drive through the Alps next up, I resorted to email. Valerie from the Colchester Town Twinning Society would have all the answers, I felt sure.

Right now, we had to cross one of the biggest mountain ranges in the world. But before we'd spotted a single peak, RG noticed a much bigger obstacle: something that might just foul up the rest of our schedule.

Rob

* * *

Valerie got back to me after our return to the UK, saying:

'I have only belonged to the Twinning Society for four years and Avignon and Colchester have been twinned for 40 years. I believe there were school exchanges before the towns were twinned. I have visited Avignon twice since I have belonged, the last being November 2011.

'We are worried about the Avignon link today. I won't go into the politics, but lady who was the link has just retired. Hopefully my husband, who has recently become Chairman, has re-established the link but it has been hard work. The flaming Health and Safety legislation has been a massive problem as Wetzlar and Avignon have always been keen on student exchanges and we are hamstrung because of this. In the "old days" members stayed with families but now it is common to stay in a hotel. Our website gives details of our last trip to Avignon plus some tasty food that was eaten!'

PART II

THE DIFFICULT
SECOND MONTH

Hi Rob,

I'm a Devon girl, born and bred. So my home town of Barnstaple seems a good choice.

My childhood memories of it include the flowerbeds on The Square that won the 'Barnstaple in Bloom' competition, year after year. The Devonian accent echoing off the vaulted ceilings of the Pannier Market. And the heat-warped candles that would work overtime in the Exmoor pubs because the generators packed up so often.

Because we lived just on the outskirts of town, we'd drive past the 'Welcome to Barnstaple' sign everyday on our way to school. I'd always wondered what the 'twinned with Uelzen in Germany, Trouville-sur-Mer in France, and Susa in Italy' bit meant. But I obviously wasn't that inquisitive as a child to go out of my way and find out.

So, for the sake of my childhood ignorance, I'd like you to visit Barnstaple's twin towns - Uelzen in Germany, Trouville-sur-Mer in France, and Susa in Italy. Or just pick your favourite.

Cheers m'dears (a typical Devon phrase),

Jo

21 · Susa
Twinned with Barnstaple
—

In which our adventurers discover their finest twinning yet

Dear Jo

Trundling down a mountain road behind a tiny white van, we remembered a twin we'd forgotten to visit. It was Montreuil-sur-mer, an almost-unpronounce-able French town we assumed was on the coast. It was one of our 45 and we'd bloody forgotten to go there.

'We'll just squeeze it in last,' said RG, the wind electrifying her hair. 'It'll be lovely – mid-summer in a little coastal French twin town. What a perfect way to end our adventure.'

'Ooh, good idea,' I said, unable to find real frustration, having just cruised through the Alps and into Italy. 'Hey, did you read Jo's message about the Pannier Market? Sounds quaint. What's a *galleria*?'

A *galleria* is a tunnel, we soon learnt from our 'AA Guide to Not Getting Killed on the Roads of Western Europe'. Italy, we'd find out, loved a tunnel. After the fourth or fifth, we curved down into the heart of sunny Susa, where schoolboys pointed at KT while their parents sat outside tiny cafés down narrow, sepia streets and enjoyed espressos and bottled beers.

Upstairs in our hotel room, RG opened the doors and stepped onto our balcony. 'You're going to like this,' she said, giggling.

In the last week, as we'd driven first through the Pyrenees then around the jagged rocks of the lower Alps, RG had fallen in love with mountains. Her breath now quickened when she spotted them looming like rhinos on the distant horizon, or stood among them as a first year stands among towering teens at school. Her eyes now smiled and focused when KT, purring, climbed steep gradients and revealed hundreds of miles of nature, untouched, unusual and unable to ever be tamed.

I stepped onto the balcony. My skin sizzled.

Below, Italian drivers were decorating the air with fancy hand gestures and tooting horns. To our left, a world of flags hung from the front of the hotel. And ahead, resting behind flats where our short-term neighbours were lunching, the Alps reminded us where we were.

'Makes you realise just how tiny we really are,' said RG, tucking into some fresh fish we'd picked up from across the road.

The two tiny adventurers finished lunch and headed out into Susa.

'Divide and conquer?' asked RG with a smile, putting on her sunglasses.

'Eh?' I asked.

'Divide and conquer. We do better like that. I go and talk to some people, you go and talk to some other people. Like in Lorient, innit.'

'Ok. Deal. You go to the town hall and I'll pop to the tourist info.'

* * *

A tiny lady, about the size of a matchstick, stood behind the counter in the tourist office.

'*Parli Inglese?*' I asked, wondering whether I was speaking the right language.

'*Scusi?*' asked the matchstick.

'*Parlez-vous... sorr... hablas ingles... no, scusi, parli—*'

'*Inglese?*' said the smiley matchstick. 'A leettle.'

Like the French, Spanish and Portuguese people we'd met who'd apologised for speaking only 'a little' English, my new Italian friend spoke a lot of English. Enough to point me towards Susa's junior school where, she promised, I'd learn about the town's relationship with Barnstaple, which you'd made sound really quite idyllic.

Away from the centre of town, Susa became less pretty but more intriguing. First, I stumbled upon Istituto Tecnico Industriale Statale Liceo Scientifico Technologico ENZO FERRARI, a school for technical bods. Then I narrowly avoided bashing my knee on a giant propeller, there to commemorate Susa's pilots who died during the Battle of the Mediterranean in October 1941.

The receptionist at Direzione Didattica Di Susa couldn't have been more Italian if he'd tried. He was the same height as Matchstick Lady and had similar tanned skin. But his was far more weathered, and his eyes were bright and alive instead of brown and alluring. His handshake was firm and his smile as pure as finest olive oil.

Sadly, he couldn't speak a word of English. Not even a little.

Walking into a primary school when you're a lost-looking man on his own gets people talking. When you can't explain your reason for being there, things get awkward. Mums start to ask questions (in Italian). I pointed and grinned at the photos of children on '*gemellaggio*' exchange visits on the walls but it only made things worse.

After a couple of minutes of trying to protest my innocence, a lady bounded down the stairs and launched into what sounded like an aggressive criticism of the secretary. He fought back, hurling invective at her. She threw her hands in the air and demanded answers. He stood as tall as a tiny man can stand.

This went on for five minutes. Then the secretary pointed at me and smiled. I shivered and closed my eyes.

Before I knew it, I was sitting in the corner of the headmaster's office with Anna Giaccone, the fierce lady at reception. I had my head down and my hands between my knees. I've never been narrower in my life.

Anna, I soon learnt, was the deputy head of the school. And, more importantly, the catalyst for Susa's twinning with Barnstaple. It was Anna who, ten years earlier, had met Frances from your hometown. The two hit it off straight away and stayed in touch, holidaying in each other's towns.

'We were good friends,' said Anna, searching the office for newspaper cuttings about the twinning. 'We get on good and we stay together. Then we speak about my school and her school and how good it is for children to visit.

'Our town is in the mountains and people don't visit much – with Torino near, it is difficult. With Barnstaple we have friends who come.'

A few years after Anna and Frances had met, Susa and Barnstaple made their friendship official. They twinned. Nothing to do with councillors or money. Friendship – to me one of the biggest positives to have ever come out of the twinning phenomenon – had won the day again.

Just as I involuntarily leant forwards to hug Anna, the office door swung open and an impeccably suited square man with perfect black hair burst in.

'Antonio,' shouted Anna, apparently furious again.

After another five minutes of chaos, which involved lots of 'Rob' and '*gemellaggio*' and 'Barnstaple', Antonio put one hand on my shoulder, smiled and offered his other hand.

'I Antonio, Roberto, and you are welcome to the school of me and Anna. *Benvenuto*, Roberto.'

'*Grazie*, Antonio,' I said, using nearly all my Italian in one excited flourish.

I left Direzione Didattica Di Susa with a big smile, a pile of photocopies of newspaper articles documenting every part of the Susa-Barnstaple story, a warmed heart, and new knowledge of Italian conversations. Raised voices and explosive hand gestures were ingredients of a casual chat, not a furious argument.

Outside Chiesa di Santa Maria Maggiore, the oldest church in Susa, I told RG about my school adventure.

'That's so amazing,' she said. 'As a well done, I'm now going to give you a tour of Susa. Just follow me.'

'Wait. How did you get on at the town hall?' I asked, as she ran off to pose under Arco di Augusto, a Roman archway built over 2000 years ago.

'Not as well as you. It was funny though – I had a similar experience to you with the secretary man. No-one spoke English so I kept saying "*Gemellaggio*" to people I saw. It's what they call twinning.'

I climbed the dusty hill to stand beside my girlfriend. 'Haha. And?'

'There was one person who could speak a little English. She asked if I was here with anyone. I said no. She said it was strange because someone else was asking about town twinning in the local school. Then it clicked – I was here with you, innit. Duh.'

'Duh-brain,' I said, giving RG a squeeze.

Follow Via Assietta downhill and trust RG's instincts and you come to Anfiteatro Romana, a 2nd-century Roman amphitheatre. While I sunned myself in the seating area upstairs, RG strolled around the arena, kicking up dust and drowning out her own voice with echoes.

'Imagine if I sent the lion in now,' I shouted down to RG.

'Dare you, meany pants,' she echoed back.

RG and I had enjoyed some battles over the last few weeks. Nothing as fiery as Italian friends discussing the weather, though. And certainly nothing as explosive as the *venationes* that once took place in *anfiteatros* like this one. These animal hunts were the Premier League clashes of their day. Animals from around the world – lions, bears, bulls and the odd hippo – would be brought to ancient Italy and pitted against local rogues. *Venationes* drew huge crowds and wiped out many thousands of the world's most beautiful creatures.

Once a few animals had been disposed of, the *venatores* would make way for the main attraction: the afternoon's gladiatorial contest, where two over-muscled chaps would try to kill each other.

Back in *centro* Susa, the sun now setting behind the *cattedrales* and *chiesas*, RG and I sat down for a tea and coffee. For the first day in what seemed like weeks, we'd forgotten about our own gladitorial fight. Instead of bickering, we discussed the beauty of your twin town and loveliness of its story.

It felt like nothing could stop us now.

Rob

Hiya Rob

A friend told me about your trip. Sounds amazing.

Please go to my twin town Frascati. I hear it's near to
Rome, where I've always wanted to visit. Tell me all
about it and then I can see if it's like home.

Good luck
Nimi

22 · Frascati
Twinned with Maidenhead
—

In which things crumble

Dear Nimi

A lot can happen in three days.

We left Susa glowing. Sunshine had toasted us, strong winds had blown away the cobwebs, and tales of town twinning and beast-slaying had fired us up for our drive to Florence, where we'd planned to relax for a couple of days.

We'd heard good things about Florence. The Uffizi with its Da Vincis, Titians, Botticellis and Caravaggios. Ponte Vecchio, the blocky medieval bridge that crosses the Arno. The statue of David overlooking Piazza della Signoria. Some of the most beautiful architecture and art in the world, we'd heard.

And I hated it.

Swarms of tourists buzzed around me, their heads down, their fingers flicking through photos of Things We Have To See – while their legs dragged them past the city's hidden treats. American, British, Japanese, Spanish, African, Indian flags hung from stalls positioned beside thousand-year-old relics. Sweaty people kept wiping their sweaty sweat on me. They were hot and bothered, arguing and pointing. Tour groups were rushing around, trying to squeeze in a million stories before their coach had to chug on to Rome for another round of Missing the Best Bits.

It was people, people, people. People in bright sunshine. People in dark shadows. People queuing in front, people queuing behind. People. People talking and shouting and swearing and sweating.

I hated it, and RG had to deal with me hating it. I tutted and sighed and hyper-ventilated and tried to hide and tried to disappear and tried to enjoy Ponte Vecchio but instead stomped along like a ten-year-old whose parents have told him he can't finish his game because dinner will get cold.

I hated it and only cheered up again when we moved on to Siena, 50 miles south of Florence, and stayed in the countryside with a beautiful man called Gianni. Gianni was short, well-built, tanned, had an endearing grasp of the English language, smiled like Tom Cruise, rode a motorbike, had a sports car and if he'd been any more woman would have given RG a run for her money.

Siena I loved. Florence? I wasn't keen. But neither of these were twinned with Maidenhead. That was Frascati, one of several hilltowns south-east of Rome.

These towns, the *Castelli Romani* or 'castles of Rome', attract Romans wanting to get away from the city. Italy's capital, we'd find, was but a distant haze from Frascati's best vantage points.

But before we even knew how close we were to Rome, we walked up and down Via Risorgimento at sunset, looking out for a guesthouse called La Porticella. After ten minutes of wandering, RG heard someone shout my name.

'Really?' I asked, looking up, causing half of Frascati to look up.

'Yeah. Someone shouted "Robert".'

The second time, I heard it too. We turned to see a young man, tall with dark hair and serious expression, walking towards us.

'Robert? Il mio nome è Paolo.'

I looked at RG and shrugged.

'*Buona sera*, Paolo,' said RG, shaking the stranger's hand.

'Hi,' I said. 'All right?'

Paolo and Sara spoke a little English. Really, a little English. RG – much better at picking up new languages than me, I'd found – worked out that La Porticella was a new venture for the young friends. Paolo had bought it to live in, but was now renting it out to make a little extra cash. They'd seen us walking past, looking lost, and knew we must be 'the British'.

Our new Italian friends accompanied us into the town to introduce us to their local speciality, porky *porchetta*, and find us a bank – so they could get their first income from their investment.

'You here vacation?' asked Paolo, towering over me. 'For good fun?'

'*Gemellaggio*,' I replied. 'Frascati and—'

'Maiden'ead,' said Sara. 'Yes. On the town signature. *Gemellato con Wind-zor and Maiden'ead*.'

'*Si, si*,' said RG. 'But in England we call it "twinning".'

Back at the house – which was more a very purple student flat – Paolo and Sara bade us *ciao-ciao* and bounced down the narrow streets in their Fiat.

'I think we're above a bar,' I said to RG, hiding behind the drapes by the bedroom window. 'Could be a noisy one tonight.'

We slept like babies, clearly exhausted after five weeks on the road, and woke the next morning to Sunday in a *Castelli Romani*. Like French, Spanish and

Portuguese towns, Italian towns did Sundays well. As we stepped onto Frascati's cobbles and walked along *via* after *via* of pastel houses, each with fewer windows than the one before, we saw nobody.

The giant playground, which had buzzed with Italian youth the evening before, was deserted. The bars, bursting with Romans just hours earlier, were now silent. Even the café where Paolo had told us we'd get breakfast echoed as we stepped inside.

'Doesn't seem like much happens in Frascati on a Sunday,' I said to RG, as we waited for our drinks and croissants. 'Wonder if Maidenhead's the same.'

RG said nothing.

'It's nice really,' I continued, 'that countries like France and Italy respect God's day. Kinda wish they would back home, too. Rather than starting electric lawnmowers at 8am.'

She wasn't even looking at me.

'Um, hello.'

'Sorry,' said RG, 'but what the fudge's happened?'

'To what?' I asked.

She pointed to the TV behind my head.

'Oh god. What's happened? Fudging hell.'

A large chunk of Italy had crumbled overnight. Statues were half their original size, *chiesas* and *cattedrales* had lost their ornaments and spires, and something had turned *vias* to rubble. Glamorous women in tight-fitting suits were telling me something about some sort of disaster, but it was lost in translation.

While RG took our bags to the car, I strolled up to a newspaper stand to find out what'd happened. But nobody could understand me. So we decided to explore Frascati before it too fell to ruin.

Maidenhead and Frascati started dating back in 1972. According to Frascati's town sign, which took us a good hour-and-a-half to track down, it was also twinned with three other towns: Bad Godesberg in Germany, the dreamy-sounding Saint-Cloud in France, and Kortrjik in Belgium.

'So it's a quintuplet,' said RG, standing in the road on a blind bend to take my photo with the sign.

'I don't think so,' I said. 'It only has a direct relationship with each of these other towns independently. If Frascati were twinned with Saint-Cloud and Bad Godesberg, and Saint-Cloud and Bad Godesberg were twinned too, then I guess they'd be triplets.'

'How do you know they're not?' asked RG.

'Good question,' I said. 'I don't.'

Back on Viale Vittoria Veneto, we sat on a bench and looked out to a distant, misty Rome.

'S'pose they can't all be as exciting as Susa,' I said to RG. 'But did you see the wifi sign earlier? At least we can get online to see what all those broken buildings are about.'

In the distance, I spotted a man selling either a broom or a novelty Roman helmet, complete with crest. His persistence was remarkable. The people of Frascati, who clearly had no use for such tat, turned him away brusquely. So he just moved on to the next person and started the whole 'You know when you're at a fancy dress party and someone asks you to sweep the floor?' line again. And again.

After ten head-down minutes of trying and failing to connect to Rome's wifi, I noticed RG had gone. I scanned the scene but Frascati had filled with people. Then, behind the three chuckling old gents, I spotted her. She was perilously close to Broomstick Man.

I jumped up, zipped my coat and headed to the rescue, still completely clueless about what'd destroyed half of Italy, but determined not to end up with Frascati's answer to the musical potato.

Rob

Hi Rob

You have to come to Swansea as it's where the film Twin Town (starring Rhys Ifans and Dougray Scott) was filmed.

Swansea's twin towns are: Aarhus (Denmark), Cork (Ireland), Ferrara (Italy), Mannheim (Germany), Nantong (China) and Pau (France).

Look forward to seeing you here!

Best Wishes

Vicki

23 · Ferrara
Twinned with Swansea

—

In which a twin is lost

Dear Vicki

What a kind invitation. Thank you.

On the drive to Ferrara, we played Guess What's Caused the Tops of Buildings to Crumble and Crush Cars Below. Ever played?

'Maybe it was a bombing,' I guessed. 'Maybe someone's really angry at the Pope. Or it's a terrorist attack. Or maybe it's just a school experiment gone wrong. Can't be too serious though, otherwise Mum would've texted to make sure we're ok.'

In our big, empty, business-break hotel outside Ferrara, we finally found the answer: there had been an *earthquake*. Yes, an earthquake. And yes, Mum had messaged to see if we were all right. But we hadn't had the signal to receive it.

'Have you been affected a lot by it?' RG asked the man at reception.

'No, it is ok. We are far from the earthquake here.'

'So it's safe to go into Ferrara? Is everything ok there?' I asked.

'Yes, it is fine,' said the towering man. 'We are maybe 60km from the middle of the earthquake, the main part.'

'That's a relief,' RG said to me in the lift. 'Would've been kind of sad to miss out on the city's best bits.'

My travelling companion had read and shared lots of exciting stuff about Ferrara before our visit – its Renaissance buildings, its galleries and museums, the quirky Ferrarese cuisine. She'd even spotted a poster for an interesting-looking art exhibition, which seemed a great way of getting to know your twin town. This would be our chance to finally get a proper dose of Italian culture. Minus the sweaty tourists of Florence and distraction of handsome Gianni in Siena.

We'd spent the previous day half-exploring the small town of Jesi, even though we'd discovered it wasn't a real twin of Devizes in Wiltshire, just a friend. Still, we paid it a visit out of curiosity and because online it had looked stunning. But in the rain and with the town hall and tourist office closed, it ended up being a non-visit, which made us all the more determined to find a stellar story behind Ferrara's relationship with Swansea.

We did the half-hour walk into the city to get a bit of exercise. Viale Cavour led us straight into the heart of Ferrara, to the Castello Estense, built in 1385 by Niccolò II d'Este.

It was a grand old castle with four meaty towers and moat and drawbridges that set it as a centrepiece for the city. Niccolò used it to keep his people at arm's length after he put in place outrageous taxes and failed to protect citizens from flooding. While they rioted, he hid in the castle. The same castle in which he had his second wife Parisina and his illegitimate son Ugo murdered because he suspected them of having an affair.

On our map, the familiar italicised 'i' for 'info' hovered smack bang in the centre of the Castello Estense. Incredibly eager all of a sudden to discover how Swansea came to be twinned with this old town, RG tried to go in.

'It's all cordoned off,' I tried to explain. 'We can't get in.'

'It's fine,' she said. 'The hotel guy said it's fine. You wait here. I'll just go over the bridge there and pop my head under. If I'm not supposed to be there, I'll just apologise and say I'm foreign. Which I am.'

And off she went.

RG didn't make it inside. Everything was police-taped off.

'Look at that tower. Something's missing,' I said to RG, pointing skywards.

She looked up, squinting.

'And that other one. Can you see it?' I added. 'It's all broken around the edges. Must be the earthquake. Y'know, the one that definitely *didn't* affect Ferrara.'

'Probably just because it's a really old building,' said RG, trying to avoid the truth. 'They must be doing maintenance work.'

Since we couldn't get to the tourist info, we settled for creating our own tour of the city. RG opened our map and circled a bunch of galleries and churches to work our way through.

There was no doubt we were approaching the Palazzo dei Diamanti as we walked up Corso Ercole D'Este. Covered from top to bottom in over 8,500 mini-pyramids, it looked just like it was made of diamonds.

'I love repetitive patterns,' said RG. 'Inside. Now. Please. Excited.'

Sigismondo d'Este, brother of the Duke Ercole I (both sons of Niccolò), had commissioned its design in 1492. The lucky man for the job was Biagio Rossetti, who set out to create a monument at the *Quadrivio degli Angeli* or 'Crossroads of the Angels' where two main roads met – Corso Ercole D'Este and Corso Porta Mare. When we visited, it was home to the National Art Gallery of Ferrara.

According to the official Palazzo dei Diamanti website, it was regarded as one of the most important Renaissance buildings in the world. Maybe if we'd managed to get inside I could tell you why. Perhaps the interior is as beautiful as the exterior. Perhaps the staff wear diamond-covered suits. Perhaps the café sells little diamond cakes that twinkle in the light.

In France, we'd got used to buildings being closed at lunchtime. Or on a Monday. And sometimes a Tuesday. But here we could see no obvious reason for the doors being chained shut, other than earthquake damage. There was just a note, which read:

IL PALAZZO DEI DIAMANTI

RIMARRA CHIUSO FINO AL TERMINE
DEI CONTROLLI STRUTTURALI

LA DIREZIONE

Rimarra? Strutturali? Chiuso? RG looked to me like a small child being denied a go on the playground swings. Sensing she needed me to come to the rescue, I checked my translation app.

'Right, it says *chiuso* means...' I tapped and swiped the screen a few times, 'ah, it means closed.'

'Ok. That's obvious because we can't get in. What do the other words mean?'

I tapped and swiped again.

'It doesn't have a translation for *stuttali*. Stupid bloody app rubbish.'

'That's because it's str*utturali*, with an "r" and "ur".'

A few more taps. 'Doesn't look good, I'm afraid. They've closed the building...

because... wait for it... bad stuff's happened.'

'Ah never mind,' said RG. 'There's another museum just around the corner from here. Let's go there.'

It was obvious what the app wanted to tell us. Ferrara was a Renaissance city, made of centuries-old architectural masterpieces. It was especially vulnerable to an earthquake. But RG wouldn't give up on her slice of culture just yet.

We strolled to the Palazzo Massari, which housed the Museum of Contemporary Arts. It was closed. So we popped over to the Palazzo Schifanoia. Closed. And all the other *palazzos* and all the *chiesas*. *Chiuso, chiuso, chiuso*. But still RG made me wander the cobbled streets in search of any sort of open building.

It was only when we got to the Basilica di Santa Maria in Vado that she finally accepted every single historical building in Ferrara – without exception – was *chiuso*. She was gutted. We'd come all this way and Nature had slapped us in the face.

We watched in silence as a team of firemen brought down the stone figure of Santa Maria. Parts of her had fallen from the top of the Basilica during the quake. The firemen were now rescuing her remains and laying her to rest in pieces.

We decided not to believe anything else the hotel man said. While RG looked up the true extent of the earthquake's damage, I did some research into the twinning with Swansea.

'Um. Oh dear,' I sighed, perched on the edge of our concrete slab bed back in the hotel. 'You should probably have a look at this.'

From my screen RG read the words 'Connection agreement with Ferrara, 1988' out loud.

'Is that their own way of describing town twinning?' she asked.

'Not quite,' I responded. 'You know how Jesi and Devizes were just "friends" and not really twins?'

'You mean Ferrara and Swansea aren't really twinned?' she asked.

I dropped my laptop to the bed and dropped my head into my hands. 'I'm afraid so. Buggering ballbags.'

Rob

Rob

There are two signs that stand either side of the single-carriage road that links the Boroughs of Bournemouth and Poole. Each sign welcomes cars through an otherwise invisible border.

I lived in Bournemouth but went to school in Poole, so we would drive past one each morning and the other every night. Welcome to Poole. Welcome to Bournemouth. When I was a bit older, I used to drive past them on my way to and from work. Things changed in both towns, but the signs stayed the same.

I remember there being quite a lot of information on the Bournemouth sign, but the only thing of genuine interest to me was the list of my home town's twins: Netanya and Lucerne. Why are these strange towns linked to mine? Who are the people that live in them? Is there a kid out there looking at a sign wondering the same things about Bournemouth?

Will you go and see what you can find for me?

Ed

24 · Lucerne

Twinned with Bournemouth

—

In which there is a dreamlike beauty

Dear Ed

I visited Bournemouth years ago for my brother's stag do. I don't remember much of your town. Or much of the weekend. Just the important bits, like the private stripshow with Crystal and the moment I sidled up to a police car down by the sea front with a man we'd all been calling the Bat. We were lost, the Bat and I. We knew we had a murky, 1970s-stained B&B to get home to but we had no idea where it was. So I knocked on the police car's window to ask for directions.

I remember the policeman waved so I waved back. He then pointed. So I pointed in the same direction and shrugged my shoulders. The policeman then told me to go away in some choice words. The next morning, I woke to news that someone from our party had urinated in the corner of their room. We packed up and left Bournemouth pretty quickly. What lovely memories.

'How long is this tunnel?' I asked RG, crossing my legs as we drove from Italy into Switzerland. 'I'm bursting.'

She looked across from the driver's seat. 'Hundred.'

'A hundred what?' I asked.

'And seven.'

'A hundred and seven what?' I asked again.

'Long?' she said, shouting over the roar of the road.

'That's really not helping. I need a wee.'

Nearly 17 kilometres. That's how long the Gotthard Strassentunnel was. Just over ten miles of two-lane traffic connecting Airolo in Italy and Goeschenen in Switzerland. Bored in 1969 to give Swiss holidaymakers an easy route into fashionable Italy, this slaloming leviathan of a road tunnel was the world's longest until the Norwegians created the 25-kilometre Laerdal Tunnel in 2000. It was an amazing human feat. Magical, breathtaking and mind-bending. Or, if you need a wee, a very long wait indeed.

We were heading for Basel, a polite town next to the German and French border where my other brother had been living for six years. This was his last month. He and his pregnant partner had decided it was time to move themselves and their baby back to England to be nearer family. We'd stay with them for a while, nipping across to Lucerne on a day trip.

'Basel,' I said to the English couple in the campervan we'd parked beside outside the Swiss end of the tunnel. 'Then Lucerne, to find out why it's twinned with Bournemouth.'

I explained the adventure to Bob and Liz.

'You must've done a few miles,' said Bob, caressing his steering wheel.

'Yeah, we started in France, little place called Douai, then drove down—'

Liz stopped me. 'We've also been a long way, haven't we, Bob? We drove down to Italy, then we're heading back up—'

'We've just been to Italy,' I said. 'Susa, Frascati, Ferrara—'

'Well we did a trip two years ago where we drove this baby all over Eastern Europe.' The caressing, now from both of them, became more intense. 'We drove almost *ten thousand miles.*'

I smiled. 'Looks like we'll just cross the ten thousand mile mark when we get back to Blighty. Probably just a bit further than *you* managed.'

And there it was. Travel Wars. One man and his wife and their campervan versus one man and his girlfriend and KT. It lasted until I realised we still had another five thousand miles or so to drive. And I still hadn't found a toilet.

* * *

It took an hour to get to your twin from Basel. We parked in a multistorey car park with tight, steep, bendy ups and downs – KT's least favourite kind.

Within five minutes of being outside the car and in the sweltering heat, we'd reached Kapellbrücke, a wooden footbridge that crossed the Reuss River. Looking up to its trussed roof, I took in the ancient paintings depicting events from Lucerne's past. Kapellbrücke, we learnt, was the oldest covered wooden bridge in Europe. Well, it will be until the Norwegians make one that's older.

It was by the bridge I lost RG. She disappeared among the throngs of people and bicycles. Another camera wielder. Another lost soul. But by now, six weeks into the trip, I'd realised just how much she'd embraced the adventure, originally my own, and could quite easily do the rest by herself. In our moments of separation, I pictured her carrying the mantle without me.

We bumped into each other again near the tourist information centre, where inside we got chatting to a young girl at the counter.

'Hello,' said RG. 'We're doing a project about twin towns. *Jumelages?*'

She looked at me to check she was speaking the right language. I had no idea. Across Switzerland, I knew the natives spoke four official languages – German, French, Italian and Romansh. Thankfully for us, the girl at the desk could speak English as well.

After a few minutes of digging around in drawers, she pulled out 'Bournemouth – Bourne without equal', a mini guide to your hometown.

'Ah, that's great,' I said. 'But we've been to Bournemouth already—'

'Oh, it is nice?' she asked.

I nodded, wondering whether to tell her about Crystal and the police incident.

After some more quizzing, we learnt there was a plaque in Lucerne that celebrated its six twinnings. Where? The giggly girl wasn't sure. Why? Again, she knew nothing. But there was definitely a plaque. Somewhere. Near some flags. She thought.

RG launched off ahead with the camera. I followed, feeling weary.

Within a few minutes, we were posing by the plaque and reading the names of Lucerne's other twins. Lucerne and Bournemouth, we found, were twinned in 1981. Though Lucerne's oldest relationship was with Murbach (or Guebwiller if you're German) in France. The 1990s saw the city connect with the States and eastern Europe. Then in 2002 Potsdam just outside Berlin became the final member of the sextet.

After walking into a red letterbox donated by the people of Bournemouth to celebrate 700 years since Switzerland was founded, we decided to explore the city and look for similarities with Bournemouth.

'Look out for strippers,' I said to RG.

We found no stripclubs. Just pebbled streets packed with people in shorts, shirts and dresses. It appeared in the 21st century, the Gotthard Strassentunnel takes as many holidaymakers from Italy into Switzerland as the other way.

We popped into a supermarket for lunch and quickly realised we couldn't afford anything. All the items were about twice the price we'd got used to paying. And we had less than half the funds we'd started the trip with. We had to eat, so I went looking for a bank to top up our funds.

That night exploring Bournemouth, I'd stumbled into many bars, a few fellow sticky-footed dancers, two enormous breasts and a police car. Today in Lucerne, after turning corner after corner, avoiding tourists, locals, builders and trams, I stumbled into something a world away.

At first, it was just a silver glint on the horizon. Then a shimmer. Then, as I walked on, I realised what I'd discovered. I sent RG a text and went running like a crazy man to find her.

'Um, I've just found something and you have to come NOW,' I said to RG, whose eyes were questioning where the money was. 'It's worth more than money. It's the most beautiful thing ever.'

'I'm not sure I've ever seen you this excited,' she said, as I grabbed her hand and yanked her through the billion people.

I'd love to tell you I'd spotted Ken Male, secretary of Bournemouth's twinning association, looking all shimmery and glinty in the blistering heat. Or Crystal, in sequinned lingerie, holidaying. But I hadn't. Instead, I'd found Lake Lucerne and its mountains. And I was almost moved to tears.

As RG and I stood on its shore, the thousands of miles of driving dissolved. Money worries fluttered away into the warm air. And any bad feelings that'd started to grow between me and my girlfriend floated towards Mount Pilatus,

2132 metres above the lake.

We were over halfway through our journey and, for the first time in weeks, back among family. The sun was shining, the mountains were stretching to the heavens and we were relaxed. Everything all of a sudden felt very right with the world. Very right indeed.

Rob

Hi Rob,

I'm from the quiet 'twinned' town Sherborne. Sherborne is part of a twinning town association called the Douzelage, where one town from each member state of Europe is twinned with Sherborne.

The aim of the Douzelage is to 'link at a grassroots level every member country of the European Union'. It is very much about strengthening the bonds with the rest of Europe. It does this by a number of means such as gatherings to discuss how to improve the economy within Europe and improve our understanding of different cultures in each twinned town.

In 2000, I and a few others went to Granville (France) where we met others from different schools from twinned towns. It was the first meeting of schools and not much was organized for us. However, one of the perks for attending Sherborne School nowadays is for this established connection with the EU twin towns and the opportunities it presents children that attend. There are so many towns from the Douzelage to visit so take your pick.

Kind regards and good luck!!

Rich

25 · Judenburg
Twinned with Sherborne

—

In which there appears an otherworldly event

Dear Rich

Tensions were high by the time we left Switzerland. With the beautiful, glimmering stillness of Lake Lucerne came glorious nature, and with glorious nature came pollen, and with pollen came hayfever. And hayfever brought with it bucketloads of tetchiness. For both of us. Soon, our agitation had spread beyond our sinuses to each other.

'Do you want to fly home? Because this isn't any bloody fun any more. For either of us. Is it?'

I'd said all this a little tipsy outside the Bird's Eye jazz club in Basel. I couldn't hold it in any longer. I had to give RG the option. And forcefully.

'Of course I don't want to go home,' she shouted back. 'I'm in this till the bitter end – it's my adventure too. You're right though. What's the point if we're just going to bicker?'

We listened to the jazz and drank our beers in silence, then broke into very serious discussions about our relationship. But two days later in Fohnsdorf, a tiny Austrian town just a stone's throw from your twin, we were giggling as I added a recent earthquake experience to a quake report website. That was the lot of twin town travellers, it seemed: at each other's throats one day, chuckling the next.

'You can't say that!' said RG, standing over my shoulder in our hotel room in Fohnsdorf.

'Why not?' I asked. 'That's exactly what it felt like. Are you sure you didn't feel it in the supermarket?'

'No. Not a thing. I was too busy trying to figure out the German word for cereal. And you can't say that cos the website's asking for a proper description of what you felt.'

'Yeah – and I proper felt the bed wobble a bit,' I said.

The bed wobbling had happened in Innsbruck, where we'd stopped for a night to break up our long drive from Basel to Judenburg. It was our second earthquake in a week. Even a country away, Italian tremors had the power to make a bed wobble a bit – and cure irritation caused by hayfever.

Back in Fohnsdorf, I hit 'submit' on earthquake-report.com and my comment was immortalised. We were staying in the town, your twin's closest (and slightly smaller) neighbour, because there seemed to be no rooms in Judenburg for the nights we needed. Which, for a small Austrian town with no major claim to fame, seemed odd.

'What's that weird sound?' RG asked, leaning into the wall.

'Is it the sound of the world gasping at my near-death experience?'

'No, listen. It sounds like... nothing I've ever heard before.'

'Earthquake number three?' I asked.

The sound was coming from the room next door. It was ethereal. Magical. Totally otherworldly. Either there was some kind of musical rehearsal happening with an unidentifiable instrument, or the third earthquake was the most mellifluous yet. The wall of our room had the words *Die Musik ist die Sprache der Lieden-schaft* written on it. I got out my translation app.

'Music is the language of the biological community,' I said.

'That explains it,' said RG, shaking her head.

Apart from Switzerland, where everyone spoke English anyway, Austria was our first venture into a German-speaking country. Neither of us had the guts yet to knock on our neighbours' door and attempt a sign language version of 'Excuse me, awfully sorry to interrupt, but we're really curious to know what it is you're playing'. So instead we dozed, the mixture of mystery music and subsiding hayfever easing us into the first night of undisturbed rest in a while.

In Judenburg's tourist office the next day, RG flicked through a booklet about the town while I stumbled over my first attempt at the word '*Partnerstadt*' since I'd stayed with Berhnard and Elke in Hoerstel. I got an apologetic look from the lady at the desk – and just a blank one from the hound sitting in the corner. Then RG remembered your brilliantly thorough message that had sent us here in the first place.

'*Douzelage?*' she asked.

That seemed to spark something in the lady's eye, and ten minutes later we were asking for Claudia Refalt at the *Rathaus*. Claudia was eager to help, though she warned us it was a Saturday, so people might not be around. In fact, we'd done well to set off as early as we had, because the *Rathaus* and tourist office were only open for half a day.

She dialled a number and became animated as she explained, I assumed, that two clueless Brits were in the office trying to find out more about Judenburg's relationship with Sherborne.

'Who do you think that man is in the coat of arms?' RG pointed at the booklet.

'Juden of Judenburg?' I suggested.

Claudia came off the phone.

'I was just speaking to the man who knows about our relationship with Sherborne.' There was hope. 'And he said he will be available on Monday to talk.' That hope was gone.

'And he's definitely not available today?' RG asked.

'I'm so sorry, he isn't. Today is the first day for the fishing season in the mountains. He has gone with his grandsons.'

By Monday, we'd be in another country.

Maybe we should've gone with your suggestion to head to Granville in France instead. Or any one of the other 24 European towns that now make up the Douzelage. Or maybe we should've just picked a day that wasn't Saturday.

The more we read about the Douzelage, the more it warmed my soul. It was heartening to know how it had strengthened bonds across Europe – and how the number of member towns had increased from the original twelve (*douze* in French) to 26 and counting. It felt like a great spin-off from town twinning, with just as important a role to play in helping people to understand different cultures and unite Europe.

Out in the Hauptplatz, the city's main square, the 75-metre-high *Stadtturm* stood over us while we figured out what to do next. That now-familiar ethereal sound coming from one of the nearby civic buildings made the decision easy.

Hackbrett. Sounds like a fish but is actually a traditional Austrian instrument from the dulcimer family. The mysterious music we'd heard the night before was teenagers rehearsing for Prima la Musica, a festival for young musicians from across the country. That explained why we couldn't get a bed in your twin.

We popped inside and stood in a far corner of a packed room, looking suspiciously like a couple of tourists trying to fit in. On stage, a tall, thin, timid-looking girl unfolded her *Hackbrett* and put it on the stand. She brought out two long sticks with what looked like a tiny elf's shoes on the end, poised herself over the instrument like a praying mantis, took a deep breath and began to play.

We stood transfixed by the sound and the way the performance was transforming her face and body. 'It reminds me of my days as a young saxophonist,' whispered RG, causing most of the room to stare at us. 'I used to take part in competitions around England. I can almost touch the nerves of these parents. They must be desperate for their children to do well. Or they just want to kill us.'

I imagined there were young people from other Douzelage member towns there. Maybe even people from Sherborne. Did you ever get the chance to hear the *Hackbrett* while at school? Do you remember?

Later, at the top of the *Stadtturm*, armed with some freshly scooped ice cream, we looked over the town to the hills beyond. Inside we found Judenburg's planetarium. We soon returned to the Hauptplatz and traced out maps of constellations on the pavement installation.

'You know, you're half right about Judenburg being named after someone called Juden,' said RG, who'd been swotting up at the tourist office. 'It means "Jews' castle". There was a massive Jewish population here back in the 13th century. But some people believe there was a medieval ruler called Jutho, who they say the city was named after. Controversial, eh?'

'Yeah – I know,' I replied. (I didn't know.) 'What other factoids have you got hidden in there?' I tapped RG's head.

'Prague is about a bajillion miles from here,' she said.

'Really? A bajillion?'

'And five.'

'Don't start that again.'

Rob

Hey Rob,

You should check out my home town Birmingham's
twin: Prague. Could be an interesting one :)

Rosie.

26 · Prague
Twinned with Birmingham

—

In which Rob has a new and unnerving experience

Dear Rosie

It was starting to seem like quite a few people had a twin town story of sorts. When we mentioned the words to the characters we met, eyes would light up and cheeks gain dimples. We found the person we were speaking to had either heard of town twinning and had no clue what it meant, knew their town had a twin but had never visited, or had once crossed the Channel to see their twin as part of a school project.

The further we drove, the more often it happened. Like in Prague. Although Christian on the bridge had never been to Birmingham, he'd once spent time in England on a school exchange. With another twin. Hence his decent English. And hence me doing that thing I did with him.

We'd driven into Prague the night before the bridge encounter. RG did half the driving, I took over as cobbled motorways turned into cobbled tramways. Other than driving around Basel to visit my brother earlier in the trip, I'd never shared a road with a tram before. And I never want to again.

'Reckon I can turn left there?' I asked RG, pointing to the road we needed.

I looked across to see her shrugging.

'Yeah?' she said, clearly less convinced of her answer than I was.

'I don't think I can.'

'No,' she agreed. 'Yep.' She smiled.

'Bloody rubbish satnav rubbish arse thing. It's not bloody working.'

'Oi,' said RG.

I put my hand on her knee. 'Not you. The bloody rubbish satnav rubbish arse thing. It's bloody rubbish. The arse.'

RG took the satnav off the windscreen and touched around the display. 'You downloaded the map with eastern Europe right?'

'Of course I did. Um, you mean there was more than one?'

As we sat in the middle of a road made up largely of tracks, a tram opposite throwing daggers at us, I froze.

'You didn't, did you? You needed to pay extra for the map with the Czech Republic on it,' said RG, putting her hand on *my* knee this time. 'Why didn't you plan this trip better, Rob? You had *ages*.'

'I was too busy dating you,' I snapped back. 'Right, I'm going to do it.'

Mirror, signal, manouev—

'TRAM!' shouted RG.

'That's what I'm wondering—'

'No, Rob, TRAM,' she screamed. 'Right next to us. Look left. Shiiiit.'

Five minutes later, we were back in exactly the same spot, having driven around in a circle to avoid being chopped in two. We'd become a sidecar, cowering in a tram's shadow as it looped around us.

'So I spoilt your adventure then?' asked RG.

'Not at all. Sorry. I'm just a bit stressed.'

In the car park later that evening, the old smiley attendant couldn't take his eyes off an unharmed KT. He gave us some sort of deal to park with him for two days – still thousands of Koruna – and we toddled off towards our budget hostel.

'Ooh, my iPod,' said RG, turning. 'Um, Rob. What's that man doing to your car?'

At breakfast the following morning, we laughed about the night before.

'I honestly thought he was breaking in to steal it,' said RG, trying her best to stomach bread that tasted like foam board. 'And when you walked up to him...'

'I just unlocked the door on the remote. Gave him the shock of his life. Serves him right for being so nosy.'

RG smiled. 'But he was speaking to his wife, right? About KT?'

'Yup. Then his mate. Apparently he'd never had a right-hand drive in his car park before. Or a sports car. Which doesn't fill me with confidence.'

It was a hot and sunny morning in Prague, so we headed straight for Charles Bridge to look for clues about its town twinning. We were there in half an hour, a now-friendly tram winding us through the industrial old streets of the city.

Terraces of pastel houses topped with terracotta-coloured pantiles on pyramid roofs lined the streets. Groups of tourists – some on foot, others on segways – criss-crossed the busy junctions. And trams tangoed on every corner.

We reached the bridge after a stroll along the river.

Charles Bridge splits Prague in two, with Staré Město and Nové Město (the old and new towns) to the east of the Vltava river, and picturesque Malá Strana (lesser town) to the west. The bridge felt like the hub – for tourists to take in jazz, culture and street art, to look up to Prague castle and to peer out along the river. Early morning and late evening, we read, the bridge was a paradise for lovers. The light would soften, tourists would leave to find cavernous restaurants and bars filled with dark beer and dumplings, and the castle would glow from its perch.

Christian, the guy from the bridge, had caught it all in the painting I'd fallen in love with.

'I think I'm going to buy it,' I whispered to RG, as we flicked through numerous bold yet melting gold, crimson, ochre and violet cityscapes.

'Do it,' she replied.

'Are you sure? I've never tried it before.'

A large man closed in on me. His Boris Johnson hair reflected the sun, while his ruddy cheeks revealed a dedication to his trade. He shook my hand.

'You like?' he asked.

RG smiled and walked away to the jazz band.

'I like,' I said. 'But the price? I don't like so much. Probably.'

Haggling, I was about to discover, was an art. One that felt very unpleasant and unnatural to me. Trevor Beattie, the man behind the Wonderbra 'Hello Boys' campaign, once advised not to haggle with a fishmonger to get a fish priced at ten pounds down to three because the fishmonger will remember you for screwing him over. Christian on Charles Bridge, if he remembers me for anything at all, will remember me as the world's worst haggler. After five minutes of chatting about twin towns, I'd fallen more in love with his painting than before. I either paid him what he was asking or more.

'Get a bargain?' asked RG, full of the joys of jazz.

'I got a story,' I replied, holding tight to my memento.

Christian was from a little town in the south of Germany. Thirteen years ago, he'd visited his UK twin town as part of a school project. He returned a few years later to work for the summer. Sadly, I couldn't understand his thick accent well enough to work out where he was from or where he visited. But he said it was 'special' and had a church.

'I asked him if he thought twinning was good,' I said to RG, as we left the bridge to find food.

'And he did?' she asked.

'Bloody loves it. He was our sort of generation, went to school just before the internet took over. So it would've been all penpals and school trips for him. None of this Facebook lark.'

After a stroll around the grounds of the castle and wander through the exquisite Renaissance collection in the gallery, we headed into a cave for a drink. It was time to dig deeper and find the real reason for Prague's twinning with Birmingham. And quaff some beer.

Full of cheap, delicious dark beer and soggy dumplings, I approached the short, slim, pretty-faced girl behind the bar.

'Hello, do you—'

'Yes,' she said, instinctively.

'Great.'

'How can I help you?' she asked.

'Birmingham,' I said.

'I am sorry,' she replied.

'Don't be. It's not your fault,' I joked.

'I mean I do not understand you. What is Birmi-ham?' she asked.

'That answers my question,' I said.

Before long, the three girls working the bar were Googling your city and trying to work out why it was twinned with theirs. They'd never heard of Birmingham and never been there. But they loved this new idea of town twinning.

It seemed a lot of the Czech Republic liked twinning. There was Sedlec-Prčice, around 50 miles south of the capital, twinned with Sutton Bridge in Lincolnshire. Náchod, near the Polish border, and Warrington. Prague itself already had 26 twins at the time of our visit, many dating back to the early 1990s when the Soviet Czechoslovakia dissolved to become the Czech Republic and Slovakia.

Following a night of jazz in the old town, we rose bright and early the next day and stuffed our pockets full of foam board in preparation for our five-hour drive across the border into Germany. There, 13 lucky twins awaited our visit.

Rob

Hiya,

I'd like you to look at Epping. Why? Because my school backed on to Epping Forest. But we were never allowed there. Too many funny goings on apparently.

Anything funny in Eppingen?

Priya

27 · Eppingen
Twinned with Epping

—

In which RG almost cries

Dear Priya

If there's one thing I wasn't expecting to find in our first German twin town, it was camels. Granted, they were performing camels, warming down after the three-day circus extravaganza Zirkus Henry, which, sadly, we'd just missed. But they were camels all the same.

We'd found them at Epping Platz – a square of grass celebrating the twinning with Epping – after a little wander around your twin.

It was a ghostly quiet Sunday in Eppingen – a complete contrast to the celebratory mood of everyone back home enjoying the Queen's pageant on the Thames. And an even bigger contrast to the nastiness that'd gone on between me and RG the afternoon before.

As hard as I was trying to ignore it, things weren't good. We'd had another argument on the drive. Something about something mean I'd said as we left Prague. Something RG had started jotting down in the car. Something I'd spotted her writing. I asked her why she couldn't just let it go.

'It's so I can be a better girlfriend in future,' she told me.

Waldbronn, Worms, the wonderfully named Neustadt an der Weinstrasse and Eppingen. Four towns in three days, then north to reach Berlin and rendezvous with friends who were visiting us.

Pulling into the driveway of Zum Strauss, our *Landgasthof* (a sort of pub-hotel-restaurant) in Waldbronn, the air had a different feel to Prague. We'd picked Waldbronn to stay for three days as it was the most central of the four twins.

'Happy to go in and tell them we're here?' I asked RG.

'Yep,' she replied, leaving the car in a flash.

Over 6,500 miles in and small talk had become a bit of a struggle. Especially after an argument that highlighted such a fundamental flaw in our partnership. But I was about to learn an excellent quick fix.

RG emerged from the little wooden hotel very slowly. 'He shouted at me,' she said, close to tears. 'Like when we got to Douai and I asked the French lady if she spoke English in English. He shouted at me, Rob.'

'Eh?'

'I said we'd booked a room and asked him if he spoke English,' she said.

'And?'

'And he shouted at me,' said RG. 'In a big German voice. Something about us being in Germany now so having to speak German. I think.'

'Oh.' I giggled.

During her altercation, RG had managed to wrestle the keys from the big man (well, that's how I imagined it). We grabbed our bag from KT and crept past the bar and upstairs to our room, locking the door behind us. The next morning, we'd left Zum Strauss before you can say *'sprechen sie Englisch?'*.

I knew Epping pretty well. One of my brothers lived there. And I'd once spent an hour trying to lift a screaming woman onto her feet from its streets, only to learn she was a habitual drunk and habitual lurer-of-young-men. That's what the police told me when I called them at 2am on a Sunday morning, a little worse for wear myself.

Eppingen had a different feel this Sunday morning, as we parked KT behind what looked like the main high street and explored.

'Very quiet,' I whispered to RG.

'Like "Hot Fuzz", innit,' she replied.

Epping and Eppingen first met and partnered back in 1981, all thanks to the Epping Forest band taking a trip south. What started as a friendship soon became official, when Epping's and Eppingen's councils joined forces. We struggled to find out exactly why the band had travelled 500 miles south-east to perform. But we guessed it had something to do with names.

According to *A History of the County of Essex*, back in the Middle Ages Epping was no more than a scattering of farms with a church beside a forest. It was the Saxons – a German tribe – who settled there. By the 17th century, the Saxons now long gone, the land had been cultivated and the forest reduced in size. Over the years, Epping developed into Epping Green, Epping Upland, Epping Heath, Epping Town, Epping Plain and Epping Forest.

Eppingen felt less varied. A bit of local research led me to discover that the '-in-gen' part of its name probably came from the Alemanni, a tribe from the upper Rhine. It meant 'place of the people of'. So, 'Eppingen' was the place of the people of Epp. Whether this Epp chap got as far as the end of the Central line and gave his name to your hometown as well is impossible to know. But I like to think he did.

(We see a hangover from Alemanni times in the way countries around the world name Germany. Go to France, for example, and it's 'Allemagne'. In Spain, it's 'Alemania'.)

Back in Eppingen, things were getting prettier. Enormous, ancient buildings were everywhere, sprouting from the earth like mighty oaks. Many dated back to the 15th century, their faces lined with criss-crossing timber. We stopped in a cute timber-framed pub for our first taste of German cuisine.

'How's your...' – RG stopped to try and work it out – 'spaghetti thing?'

'Completely cold. And a bit like spaghetti, except it's some sort of *fleisch*. On some sort of salad. Nice beer though.'

After a stroll through town, we came to a stone statue of two people embracing. With a little deciphering of signs, we worked out it was there to celebrate another of Eppingen's twinning relationships. This time with Szigetvár in Hungary. We were standing on Szigetvár Platz.

'If there's a Szigetvár Platz, there's bound to be an Epping Platz,' said RG.

Within twenty minutes, we were staring at camels on Epping Platz, discussing how if camels could talk we were sure they would've been telling us what a cracking time the town had had at Zirkus Henry. We strolled back to the car, chuffed to have found a mention of Epping in Eppingen. It took me back to seeing Waltham-Abbey-Platz in my own twin town, Hoerstel. I had a big grin on my face.

In Waldbronn, we slipped upstairs unnoticed and checked out the Epping-Eppingen twinning website. We found it was one of the liveliest twinnings out there. Year to year, residents of both towns liked to visit one another's homes on exchanges and to put on local markets. Head to Epping market at the right time and you might be lucky enough to sample some cold *fleisch* spaghetti on some sort of salad.

In Epping, you'd definitely find twinning-themed language courses, quiz nights and even the occasional magic evening, if you're lucky. All to fund town twinning and keep the flame flickering.

'That's lovely, isn' it? The effort they're putting in to keep it all going,' I said to RG, perched on the edge of the bed.

'Yes. Bloody lovely. Shall we go and celebrate?' she replied.

'You have an idea?' I asked.

'Of course.'

Rob

Rob

My home town of St Albans is twinned with Worms, Germany. Yes, Worms. As in the Diet of. Look it up. I went there once on a school trip for the similarly pointless reason that you may go – because of the twin thing. If the idea of sampling the Diet of Worms does not tempt you, I don't know what will.

Good luck.

Simon

28 · Worms
Twinned with St Albans
—

In which there is a separation

Dear Simon

City of variety. City of religions. City of wine. City of the Nibelungen. Take your pick. You see, according to the tourist office in your twin town, you can get just about anything in Worms. Possibly even a diet of worms.

RG and I had just a morning there to suss out its story. So we made a plan. Quick wander, look at the famous cathedral, pop to the *Rathaus* for a chat with the *Burgermeister* then shoot off to the fanciest-sounding town on the whole trip.

Easy.

'I say we split,' I said to RG, reversing into a parking space near the town centre.

'Deal. Where are the papers?'

'Oh ha-di-ha,' I said. 'At some point, I'll head to the town hall, you go suss out the other bits. Divide and conquer. Deal?'

'Deal,' she replied.

'Right, let's see this cathedral.'

It'd be tricky to miss St Peter's Cathedral. The smallest of the three Romanesque imperial cathedrals on the Rhine, it was still fairly gigantic. First thing we noticed were the four towers, shooting to the sky like fuel tanks of a shuttle rocket. Then it was that rose window, with its pretty petals pointing in.

'Let's have a look inside,' said RG.

'Let's look around town and *then* go in,' I suggested.

'Sure?' she asked.

'I'd love to do the research first, then have the fun. Why don't we walk around, see what we can find, go to the *Rathaus*, then look in the cathedral?' I said.

'Because we won't have time,' said RG. 'We never have time.'

'Then we'll *make* time.'

True to form, I ran out of time to look around Worms cathedral. RG, determined not to let me stop her doing what she wanted to do, had headed in. I'd made my way to the *Rathaus* instead, for what would be my first attempt at withdrawing *Partnerschaft* information from a German person since Hoerstel. But this time I had no Varnskuehlers in support.

The slender lady at reception didn't speak English.

'Um, I'm... *je sui*... no... *nein*... *Ich habe*... Um... *Stadt*. Information *fur votre stadt*,' I stuttered.

She laughed a fine double-burst laugh and disappeared behind her desk.

'Hello?' I said.

'Hallo,' came her voice from under the reception.

I stood for about thirty seconds, imagining the cage she kept under her desk.

The place where all receptionists were urged to retreat in times of panic. 'Hello,' I tried one last time.

Up she popped, like a Jack-in-the-box.

'Hallo,' she said, offering me a leaflet called 'Worms – City of variety'. 'Ex-peri-ence and cele-brat,' she read from the front cover. '*Lesen*. For you. *Lesen*.'

I smiled. 'A very good lesson, I'm sure. But I'm here for your... *Partnerschaft*.'

Back down she went. This time returning with 'Worms – City of religions'.

'*Partnerschaft?*' I asked again.

From under 'Worms – City of religions', she produced 'Worms – City of wine'.

'Worms – city twinned with St Albans in England?' I asked.

'Ohhhhhh, Saint Alban,' she said. '*Nein. Entschuldigung. Danke.*'

I left the *Rathaus* trying to work out what this brilliantly German word meant. '*Entschuldigung*,' I said, walking up to the doors of St Peter's. '*Entschuldigung*,' I said, strolling around Eis Vannini, probably the biggest ice cream van in exist-ence. '*Entschuldigung*,' I said, bumping into RG on Markplatz.

'Ohmydays – that's amazing,' she said, beaming.

'There are two bigger ones down the Rhine,' I said. 'Stunning, eh?'

'No, the ice cream van. Eis Vannini. Ice cream for lunch?'

'Really?' I asked.

'No, course not,' she said. 'Unless *you* want it...'

The most intriguing of the leaflets the lady in the town hall had handed me was the one about the Nibelungen. As we started to walk out of your twin – having failed to find its *Partnerschaft* story – I tried to retell the myth of the Nibelungen to RG.

'Some say they were dwarves. Others say there were just a mythical people. Either way, they were the Nibelungos, and story has it they settled in Worms in the 5th century.'

'Nibe-lungos? Some say that sounds like the female version of a blow-ee...'

'You never take my stories seriously,' I whined.

'You're just jealous I'm funnier than you, innit,' said RG.

'Not a competition, so... And you're not. I'm well funnier. Like times ten.'

'Stupider, more like. Shall we go to the Jewish cemetery?' she asked.

'What about the Nibelungen?'

As we neared the Jewish cemetery – one of the oldest of its kind in Europe – I tried to finish the story for RG. 'And there was a bloke called Seigfried and he rescued Kriemhild from the Kuperan and then I think he fed himself to the dragon to save the city. The end.'

'Have you ever thought about writing books, my love?' my girlfriend joked.

The evening before, RG and I had celebrated Epping's successful twinning story with a couple of local Palmbraus beers and schnitzels in Zum Strauss. Books had come up in conversation. RG said I should stick all our stories together and become a famous travel writer. And what would she do?

'I think I want to leave my job, Rob. I think I want a new challenge in life.'

As soon as we stepped inside Heiliger Sand, we went silent. With the earliest gravestone dated at 1076, and the final body buried there in 1911, this sacred ground had over 800 years of stories below its surface.

As we continued to walk, we reached the graves of Rabbi Meir of Rothenburg and Alexander Ben Solomon Wimpfen Sükind. Both were covered in little pieces of paper, kept down by stones. These were the venerated two. One died a martyr, forbidding his followers from paying his ransom. While the other – through respect – ransomed the rabbi's corpse and brought it to Heiliger Sand. The two men now rest side by side.

We said nothing back up the hill to KT. I can't tell you what RG was thinking, but I was wondering about the fate of the the two twin town adventurers, now over halfway through their adventure. Either barely talking, or always treading on eggshells, we'd travelled thousands of miles together and managed to drift many miles apart. *If we were to die now*, I thought, *would they bury us together? And if they did, would RG find a way of burrowing to a more favourable final resting place?*

'Time to move on, my dear?' I asked.

RG quarter-smiled. 'Let us.'

Rob

Rob

I come from Lincoln, and we're twinned with Neustadt an der Weinstrasse in Germany. The partnership started up in 1969, and in 1982 Neustadt brought their Christmas market to Lincoln. Lincoln's now got one of the biggest Christmas Markets in Europe! And coachloads of people from Neustadt come every year.

But what's it like there? I have no idea.

Abby

29 · Neustadt an der Weinstrasse Twinned with Lincoln

—

In which RG's mind wanders to other things

Dear Abby

'So, Ana gets to Berlin around now,' said RG.

She'd turned our twinning schedule over and was scribbling on the reverse.

'In fact, she's probably already there. In fact—' looking through her messages, 'yep, she's been there a couple of days already. With Lizzie. When does Ed get there?'

'Is Ed coming?' I asked.

'You know Ed's coming. The girls invited him. And you invited him. Lads and bants and football and all that crap. I mean... loveliness,' said RG.

She started scribbling through the scribbles. 'We've got options. Squeeze in Giessen, Goettingen and Uelzen between now and Berlin, which would probably mean leaving yesterday...'

'Great. And the other option?' I asked.

RG cleared her throat. 'Waldbronn tomorrow, five-hour drive across Germany to Chemnitz, three hours over to Berlin. Get there later Thursday, meet the gang. Spend... one, two, three, four... four and a half days there.'

'Any benefits of doing it that way?' I asked.

RG turned to me from KT's passenger seat. 'Yeah. It's possible that way.'

In five minutes, our next week was planned. Which meant we could get the most out of your twin. A town, you told us, that had a pretty active relationship with your hometown, Lincoln.

'Abby says it started in 1969, and in 1982 Neustadt took their Christmas market to Lincoln,' I told RG. 'And now Lincoln's got one of the biggest Christmas markets in Europe. Bloody hell. And, and I quote, coachloads of people from Neustadt come every year. Exciting.'

After Eppingen and Worms – both charming in their own special way – I can't say we were too excited by the prospect of a third German twin in two days. Every little town we drove through looked the same. The men were old and rotund, the women were old and a little less rotund. Apart from the odd camel, not much seemed to change from town to town. Then we wandered into Neustadt an der Weinstrasse.

Tiny, winding and wonderful, the streets of your twin connected like the tunnels of an ant colony. We'd picked up a map from the *Tourist Information* (words we recognised) and, on spreading it out, we noticed the thoughtful people of Neustadt had created a short tour of the colony. We started at The Saalbau, Neustadt's convention centre, which was across the road from the tourist info. And we were lost by two, The Stork's Tower.

But what a place to get lost. Not even 30,000 people lived in Germany's 'secret wine capital'. It sat on the edge of the Palatinate Forest, which covered over 1700 square kilometres (roughly 650 square miles).

'Did you read that thing about Lincoln and wine?' asked RG.

'Um. No. What thing?'

Back in our *Landgasthof* the night before, RG had been doing some first-class research. She'd discovered that Lincoln once had a vineyard. It was in the medieval Bishop's Palace – and was planted in 1972 with grapes from Neustadt. In 2012, with the landscaping of the garden, the vineyard once again got a new lease of life. It was now looked after by a lady called Samantha and other people in her community project.

'Did you know that although migrant storks have returned to Neustadt, they haven't yet chosen the old fortified tower as their preferred accommodation?' my guide explained, very convincingly.

'Ain't you just bursting with facts this morning?' I said to RG.

It seems unfair to rank twin towns based on very quick visits to each. Of the 29 we'd seen so far, every one had had its own charm. The blustery beaches of our Bretagne towns in those first weeks. Port evening in Porto. The shimmering lake of Lucerne. Crumbling Ferrara, picturesque Prague. But what splished and splashed around the next corner might just have been the most perfect moment of the trip for me.

'What the *Entschuldigung?*' I exclaimed.

RG looked at me, confused. 'What the *sorry?*' she questioned.

'Ohhhhhhh, *that's* what it means.'

'What did you think it meant?' asked RG.

I shrugged.

'Have you heard people saying "*Tschuss*" too?' she went on.

'I think you mean "juice", my dear.'

'Look,' said RG, changing subject like you might with an annoying toddler, 'those half-bird, half-animal creatures are having a waterfight. Cool, huh?'

We'd reached number four on the tour – the Eldwedritsche Brunnen. A fountain based on the myth that gave Neustadt its fun and carefree feel. As RG had pointed out, these Eldwedritsche were half-bird, half-animal but with human expressions. Folklore placed them in the Palatinate Forest – they were cryptids, rumoured but never proven to exist.

Hitting the Mittelgasse and Hintergasse, numbers five and seven on the tour, we discovered Neustadt at its most pretty. We found taverns, restaurants, art galleries, boutiques, and vegetation that belonged on the Mediterranean all living below the looming forest. It was easy to imagine the beady eyes of the Eldwedritsche, blinking in the shadows.

With feet raw and minds overflowing with learning, we stopped at a little café just off the Markplatz, dubbed the historic centre of Neustadt. We sat quietly with a coffee and a hot chocolate, each reading our own leaflet. RG continued to flick the pages of the charmingly translated 'Tour of the town together street-map', while I laid out the guide to Lincoln we'd picked up earlier.

'Think the lady in the tourist office thought we were planning a trip to Lincoln,' I said to RG. 'It's in German, too, which is a bit of a bugger.'

From what I could decipher, Lincoln was a place in England with two thousand somethings. It had a Roman arch called the Newport Arch, and there was a museum dedicated to Usher. William invaded Lincoln and did something to the cathedral (possibly built it). And there was a park with an old lady who liked to feed ducks. You, or she, could have a coffee or a picnic there.

We didn't make it inside the 18th century *Rathaus*. It looked stunning, standing there at the edge of the market square, a subtle cream and sandstone. All we had energy for was *Flammekueche* (like pizza, but a billion times tastier) and some local wine, which went down a treat.

'Waldbronn, Chemnitz, Berlin?' I asked RG, as we ducked inside to avoid some dollops of rain.

'Yep. And I think it's pronounced Kem-nitz. Not *shem*,' she replied.

'Cool. Looking forward to it?' I asked.

'Yep. Berlin should be great,' she said.

Rob

Rob

My friend Anita got in touch. She told me about your
mad trip.

She says she sent you to our twin town Carbonne
(I've been and loved it). So am I allowed to send you to
Monmouth's other twin, Waldbronn in Germany? Never
been there. I want to know if it's like here or Carbonne.

Pretty please...

Manny

30 · Waldbronn
Twinned with Monmouth

—

In which there is a movie moment

Dear Manny

In 2011, Waldbronn and Monmouth celebrated their 25th twinning anniversary.

Over those 25 years, the towns achieved a lot together. Barbeques, cycle trips, boating adventures, camel rides. Flower beds were planted, morris men made merry, plaques were stuck to stones, red telephone boxes were installed, and markets were shared. All thanks to twinning. Waldbronn and Monmouth, we discovered, were around 630 miles apart. Yet, for the last quarter of a century, they'd shared a history. Though if it hadn't been for one man called John, things could've turned out very different.

'Looks like we walk into town,' said RG, 'then out of town, to another town, then to another town, then maybe one more town. Then we get back here.'

We were looking at a map of the area.

We'd found out from our landlord Scary Frank – who was actually big, bubbly and just couldn't speak English – that we weren't actually staying in Waldbronn. Landgasthof Zum Strauss was in Etzenrot, one the smaller towns that made up the Waldbronn collection. To get to the main attraction, we needed to walk.

A narrow wooded lane took us from Etzenrot to Waldbronn proper, where we had high hopes of finding the *Rathaus* and hearing stories. The lane was lovely, and the playing field it crossed and swings we laughed on were fun. But we sensed there was more.

Then there it was, 'Monmouthplatz' on a street sign, beside a stone displaying a plaque that announced:

Waldbronn-Monmouth (Wales)
Partnerschaft
Seit 1986, Km 1020

We glanced at each other and smiled.

'Ooh, look,' said RG, running towards the red telephone box. 'Take my photo inside. Take my photo inside. Please.'

It was early June in Germany and cold. The sunshine of eastern Spain, the south of France, Italy and beautiful Lucerne had left us long ago. Rain jackets and jeans were our friends once again. As was the map of Europe I'd managed to download onto my phone in Austria. Although it'd missed our street in Prague and sent us into Praha 1 and tramageddon, it'd since proved invaluable on the streets of different twins.

'So, where's the *Rathaus*, lady?' I asked RG, who was holding my phone.

She shrugged. 'Seems we've hardly scratched the surface. If it's not here, it's probably in Busenbach or Reichenbach or Neurod. Like you were telling me about Hoerstel, together they must all make up the town of Waldbronn.'

We walked a circuit of Waldbronn to find the story we needed. We eventually came across an excellent one inside a brochure designed to celebrate the 25th anniversaries of Waldbronn's twinnings with Monmouth and Saint-Gervais in the French Alps. I got my copy from Gertrud, trusted *Sekretariat* of Franz Masino, *Burgermeister* extraordinaire. Franz, sadly, was out and about when I popped into the *Rathaus* – lost, no doubt, somewhere between one neighbourhood and the next.

The inside walls of the town hall – which felt more like a hospital than civic and cultural hub – were lined with twinning certificates. Each was headed in ornate blackletter, then penned in a florid, calligraphic hand. I imagined the language matched the beauty of the script itself. But John Oswald, he was the man who'd made all this possible.

Back in 1985, Mr Oswald was asked by someone from Monmouth Town Council to suggest a good twin. A town in Germany, ideally. At the time, a few towns near Karlsruhe in the south-east were looking to pair up. So the county council gave John a list to see which he thought would be the best fit. After failing to pinpoint any on his atlas, he called the phone number on the list.

At the time, new communities like Waldbronn were being created. Waldbronn itself was a coming together of Busenbach and Reichenbach, the latter having merged with Etzenrot a year earlier. This idea intrigued John, who did a little more research. He wanted a mix: somewhere similar to Monmouth but with enough differences to pique people's interest. Waldbronn was the answer.

I read this in a café in Busenbach, where RG got a step closer to ice cream for lunch. Instead, we went for cake. Big cake. Big, creamy, German cake. The sort that would've made Bernhard and Elke very proud.

'It's a great story,' said RG. 'One of the best so far. Makes me feel warm in my heart. Like this big, creamy, German cake.'

Soon, the towns had twinning committees, interested citizens were hopping back and forth between the countries, and a year later everything was official. Your hometown and Waldbronn, the new town, were twins.

'So, *Shem*-nitz—' I said to RG, an avalanche of fake cream dripping down my chin.

'*Kem*-nitz,' corrected RG. 'Like I said last time.'

'Whatever. How far?' I asked.

'It'll take around five hours with a stop. It's about 500 kilometres.'

We took our time on the wander back to Etzenrot. After all, what was an extra ten minutes on a five-hour journey? Halfway there, the sun broke through and shot golden rays down upon us as we walked side by side, chilly hand in chilly hand.

In the centre of town, I went for a wander while RG picked up supplies. And everything just looked a bit... new. Now and then, some timber-framed cabins caught my eye, but most of the town looked a bit... new. Get outside the town and hit the forests and find the rivers and Waldbronn becomes another world. But here, now, strolling the streets, I was ready to leave.

'We need petrol,' I said to RG, after we'd both said farewell to Frank, the lovely giant from our *Landgasthof*.

RG set up the satnav. 'This thing should tell us where a petrol station is.'

We pulled away.

'We walked down here earlier,' I said to RG, as our electronic guide took us back to Monmouthplatz. 'Didn't see any petrol stations.'

She shrugged. 'Maybe it's reallllly tiny, with tiny people and tiny pumps and—'

Then, in a moment from the movies, the world's smallest petrol station loomed tiny on the side of the road. RG stopped mid-quip.

'Is that...' I started.

My girlfriend, almost falling across my lap and out of the door to look closer, read the sign: 'That's Franz Vogel's Tiny Tiny Petrol Station.'

'Is that what it says?' I asked, driving past.

'No. Obviously. Hey, why are we driving on? Thought you said we needed petrol.'

'We do,' I replied. 'But not tiny petrol.'

Rob

Hi Rob

Chemnitz please, or Karl Marx Stadt as I think it used to be known. If that name's not enough to get you curious, then I don't know what is.

I'm from Manchester.

Rowena

31 · Chemnitz
Twinned with Manchester
—

In which Rob discovers a distant and deceased companion

Dear Rowena

Karl Marx was quite a man. As the Industrial Revolution kicked in around Europe, and the gulf between those with money and those who served those with money grew, he decided to do something. He was cheesed off. *It just isn't right*, he thought. *The world should be a fairer place. Somewhere stateless and classless.*

Marx put all his thoughts – and a few from the handsomely bearded Friedrich Engels – down in a short book. It was *Das Kommunistische Manifest*, or *The Communist Manifesto*. He was just 30 years old.

In the heart of Chemnitz, we came across a seven metre tall stone statue of Karl Marx's head. It was there in remembrance of the man and of the time your twin was called Karl-Marx-Stadt. His cheeks, jaw, wide beard and bags under his eyes were severely angled. They surrounded the smooth dome of his head. His was the face of complete determination, unwavering belief and, some say (including Engels), genius.

While we were there, Chemnitz was describing itself as a 'charming' city and the 'City of Modernity'. According to a booklet 'at first sight its "face" is perhaps a little bit austere, but then it becomes more and more friendly'. A bit like Marx himself, I decided.

'I wonder what a town twinning manifesto would look like,' I said to RG, as we sat on the city-bound tram from our out-of-town hotel. 'I like the idea we're all equals in the land of twins. Here to get to know and help one another.'

'That's how it *should* be,' said RG, peering outside as the outskirts of your twin passed us by. 'I think we're learning it's not quite working like that though.'

During the drive from Waldbronn, we'd crossed from west to east Germany, from the former Federal Republic into the former German Democratic Republic. We were now in the land the Soviets had occupied. A place where the Marxist dream had turned sour.

'Cake?' I asked RG, as we slalomed between locals in the busy market.

My travelling companion had decided today would be a writing day. A chance for her to take the weight off and relax. As we kissed goodbye, I realised this would be the first time in weeks that my girlfriend and I would be apart.

Walking along the shaded city centre street, I didn't look back. But before I could process everything that'd been said and done recently, I tripped over a penguin. I tried to read the plaque. *Travel a long way south from Chemnitz and you'll reach Antarctica,* it seemed to suggest. *Also, look at the map of Antarctica and you'll notice it's the same shape as Chemnitz. So we've put some Emperor penguins here to celebrate all this.*

A man came and stood beside me and spoke something in German.

'*Entschuldigung,*' I tried for the first time proper. '*Iche—*'

'You're an Englander?' he said. 'I like you. You enjoy our penguins?'

I explained I loved his penguins. That I'd come from England and felt lucky to have seen his penguins, all this way north of their home in the Antarctic. He laughed and said he found me funny. He found all Englanders funny, he said. I thought back to Bernhard and Elke saying something similar.

Wherever we went, whoever we bumped into, this single strain of humanness showed its pretty head over again. Whatever the weather, a warmth came from being in the middle of a local town, surrounded by local people. Never aliens, never outsiders – by now, almost two months into our travels, we were brothers and sisters. It seemed obvious we all just wanted to get along.

Outside the city centre, past the statue of Marx, away from the big, shiny, modern buildings, beyond the penguins, I found a park with a lake. As I sat on a bench facing the city, smiling joggers bounced by. A mum pushed her tiny baby-in-buggy through the gate. Two businessmen guffawed. A duck flew over and splash-landed in the water. And a couple of young teens played.

Me? I sat staring at my phone, questioning who I was and what I was putting this poor girl through. It was a grotesque display of self-indulgence and self-analysis. It turned into a poem of admittance. I admitted to myself for the first time that she'd be better off with somebody else. Then I did a little manly cry.

Later in the day I found RG exactly where I'd left her, still scribbling away in her notepad.

'Any more notes about me in there?' I quipped, then instantly regretted. 'ONLY JOKING.'

The next morning, we drove back into the city and left the car by the park. I'd told RG how beautiful I'd found it there and she was keen to see it. While she sat on a park bench near where I'd shared my soul (with myself), I headed back into Chemnitz to track down twinning stories. But all I found was half a cooked chicken, which I bought from a Chinese man and his mum.

Just like the day before, I passed Marx, who was looking down on me like an angry headteacher.

Karl Marx was never one to fit in with society. In just two semesters at Bonn University, he'd been put in prison for drunkenness and disturbing the peace, he'd got himself into debt, and he'd been part of a duel with the Borussia Corps, an early university fraternity. Because of this, Marx's father had decided Bonn probably wasn't the right environment for his son, so moved him to the University of Berlin, a more serious establishment.

Marx soon became less a fighter and more a political radical. He was living in Brussels when he published *Das Kommunistische Manifest*. (A year later, in 1849, he was thrown out of Belgium.)

In 1867, a more measured Marx, now living in London, published *Das Kapital*. This was his study of capitalism and all its wiles, as he saw it. He still believed that the under classes would one day rise up again the capitalist way.

Marx died in north London in 1883. He never got to see his revolutionary theories put to the test. The large tombstone erected by the communist party of Great Britain in 1954 was etched with the last line of his manifesto: 'Workers of all lands unite'.

We left Chemnitz in the early afternoon and headed for Germany's capital. Although not one of our twins, this city would help guide the rest of our adventure, like it had guided the rest of Karl Marx's life.

As we drove away from your twin, I thought about Marx's life travelling around the Continent. I wondered what he would've made of town twinning, and mine and RG's little adventure.

Rob

Dear Rob

I was born in Barnstaple in Devon but I've moved to Bristol.
I always remember reading about a place that was our 'twin
town' called Uelzen. I think a friend from school went there
once. Would you go? Do I qualify? I'm intrigued by this
town twinning thing. Tell me stories...

Yours, Adrian

32 · Uelzen
Twinned with Barnstaple
—

In which Rob almost pays for his stubbornness

Dear Adrian

There was a blinding flash.

'Bollocks,' I shouted.

'Where? I mean what?' asked RG.

'Balls, balls, bloody massive balls. Just got flashed by some bastard speed camera. Bloody hell. Wonder what that means.'

RG slapped me on the thigh. 'That you were speeding, my little Etzenrot.'

We pulled into the car park of our guesthouse, which, as was getting quite common in Germany, was in the middle of nowhere. In the lobby, the chubby-cheeked son of the owner got excited about speaking English with us. 'You are – what you call it? – the fans of the football, jah?' he asked, looking like he wanted to high-five himself.

'Yes, yes. It is a big game for England on Friday,' I said. 'Sweden.'

He laughed. 'Yes, yes. England. I think you say you haven't a hope in hell, jah? But Germany. We are better. We play the Netherlands tomorrow. We will win. You will go and support my team, jah?'

Twenty minutes later, we were sitting in our little room wearing sweaty Germany scarves our new friend had found for us in his bedroom. 'Football is coming home, jah?' He shut us in.

'You know what, jah?' I said to RG. 'I'm going to go for a walk in the morning. Into town. Find my own way. Is that cool, jah?'

'Yeah, of course. Sounds like a right little treat to me. But please drop the silly accent.' She kissed me. 'Love you.'

On the walk through the forest the next morning, I found myself wearing a stupid smile. I grinned at and *guten-tag'd* everyone I saw. Which was one confused farmer. I chatted with the trees, toyed with the grass and wished away the wispy cloud with happy whistles. In Berlin, RG and I had shared that we worried we weren't right for each other and then decided to brush it under the carpet. In that moment, a great weight had lifted from my shoulders.

As another twig clicked under my heels, I thought back to watching some of the European football championships with a beer, and our friends Ed, Ana and Lizzie. As we all bantered about nothing, petty fallings out had floated away with wafts of Berlin wurst. On a surface level, RG and I could still appear to be the perfect team.

Skipping through the forest, I felt like Little Red Riding Hood.

A text arrived from RG. 'Hope you're having fun, my love. I'll be ready to drive in soon. Probably be there in an hour. Promise to look after KT. Tschuss/juice x.'

Just as I was about to reply, I heard little voices in the distance. Giggling, shouting, screaming. And, most ominously, I heard splashing. With every step I took, the ground got soggier. I checked my phone map and couldn't spot anything out of the ordinary. 'Ok, my dear. I'm just...' I started to reply.

Then I saw the pony. In a fast-flowing but what looked like shallow stream.

And kids – a school group, out for the morning, with their pony. Down by the shallow stream. Kids. And their pony. All by the stream.

Forty-five minutes I waited opposite the children. Forty-five minutes trying to work out what to do, knowing – because of my stubbornness – going back wasn't an option. Forty-five minutes I waited for the group to leave. Eventually, they did. But not before one of the little boys went to step further than a foot into the water and his teacher yanked him back hard by the arm.

She shouted at him. He cried.

I finished my text to RG. 'Ok, my dear. I'm just on my way in, too. It'll be fine – don't worry. See you in a bit x.'

Uelzen is equidistant from Hamburg and Bremmen, bang in the middle of northern Germany. It was once a member of the Hanseatic League, which was founded in the 12th century to ease the passage of merchants through this part of Germany and the Baltic. Back in the Middle Ages, travelling with goods was a treacherous business. Hence the setting up of a confederation to protect economic interests and diplomatic privileges along trade routes. I learnt all this from my phone, while waiting for my moment to cross the stream. Thinking back, I probably looked like I was taking photos of the kids.

Halfway across, dressed in nothing but boxers and a t-shirt, I regretted my stubbornness and wished for a confederation that would protect idiots along Germany's wet routes. The water was freezing. Tiny stones shot up into my soles with every tentative step. I wondered whether to message RG a goodbye. Then another splash smacked me back into real life and I tip-toed on, shredding my feet.

On the opposite bank, I stretched back and dried my legs in the sun. Another message came in. 'What are you up to?' it said.

* * *

When asked about Uelzen's relationship with Barnstaple, the young man in the tourist office would say just one thing: 'You know the buyer of owls?' With RG waiting for me on the *Platz* outside, I kept insisting that no, I didn't, but I really wanted to know something about the *Partnerschaft*.

'I will copy you some of the information,' he said, ten minutes later.

'Great. *Danke. Danke schoen.*'

Outside, I handed RG the piece of A4 paper the young man had given me. She looked over it, eyebrows raised. She then read through. 'Owls? That's great, sugar. But what about Barnstaple and town twinning? And what did you mean in your text earlier?'

We found two statues in Uelzen that celebrated the buyer of owls story. One was carved beautifully in wood and depicted three owls, two large and sitting sentinel above a smaller third. The other was metal and seemed a closer representation of the story. We grabbed a delicious Thüringer sausage from a friendly local in the market and headed to the wooden owls for photos.

'Hey, do you know the buyer of owls?' shouted the sausage seller behind us.

We turned and gave him the thumbs up.

Where Devon has its Hairy Hands and Devil's Footprints, Uelzen's favourite piece of local lore concerns a peasant, a merchant and three young owls.

One peaceful Sunday morning – let's imagine around the time when the Hanseatic League was in full swing – a peasant was ambling into town with a sack over his shoulder. A merchant noticed the sack moving.

'What have you got in that sack, mein Herr?' asked the merchant.

'Some without socks,' answered the peasant.

'Heathcocks? Brilliant. I bloody love heathcocks,' said the merchant, getting out his wallet. 'How much do you want for them?'

'For these some without socks?' asked the peasant.

'Yep. How much?'

The merchant handed over a lot of cash and headed off, happy with his bargain.

(For this to work, you need to know 'some without socks' in Low German is *Barftgaans*, while 'heathcocks' is *Barkhahns*. You also need to know heathcocks were old game birds, much sought after at the time. And finally you need to stop questioning why someone would describe anything as 'some without socks'.)

Anyway, that all happened and the merchant went home. When he opened the sack he was furious. Instead of heathcocks, three owls flew out. *WTF?* he thought, and went to see the mayor.

The mayor brought the peasant and merchant together.

'I'm suing you,' the merchant shouted at the peasant. 'You said these were heathcocks.'

'No, no, no,' replied the peasant, calmly, 'I said they were *some without socks*. Completely different things. Although, nobody can deny the fact that night and day owls walk barefoot – without shoes and stockings.'

The mayor laughed a hearty laugh and said the peasant had a point. The merchant had no leg to stand on. Just a few owls.

Dozing off to sleep in a park across the little bridge from the market, having wandered your twin for a couple of hours and found it very pretty, small and charming, RG and I giggled about the buyer of owls.

'I can't wait to tell people that story when we get home,' she said.

'People. Will. Love it,' I said. 'I bet they'll giggle about me and the stream, too.'

'What stream?' asked RG.

Rob

Rob

Vicki told me about your trip. Enjoy it!

If you're going all the way to Italy, you might as well swing
by Aarhus, too. It's just a bit further north in Denmark (hehe).
If you go, let me know what you find! Can't be as pretty
as Swansea...

Gwen

33 · Aarhus
Twinned with Swansea

—

In which there is a sobering realisation

Dear Gwen

RG couldn't believe I'd waded through that stream in Uelzen. Until I reminded her about my stubbornness and desire to never turn back on myself in life, like in Avignon. Then she said it all made sense. And that I was mad.

'As mad as a bag of owls?' I asked, as we crossed the border into Denmark.

You need an excuse to go to Denmark, I'd always thought. Other than Copenhagen, most people I knew would have struggled to name another part of this long country, which reaches up like a flame from the top of Germany. It's sad, because – as we discovered during our five days there – it's full of history, culture, beautiful people and strong-smelling fish.

We hadn't booked anywhere to stay in Aarhus. With so much experience of trying our luck, we thought we wouldn't need to. There'd be a lovely cottage by the harbour, run by an elderly Danish couple, Viggo and Anja, and their elkhound, Thor. Viggo would've been down to the harbour in the morning to pick us up some fresh seafood, while Anja, just as we turned up, would be getting the fire going.

I rubbed my hands in expectation as we walked into a bar.

'Hello, do you speak English?' we asked a short-haired, sweet-faced, chubby-cheeked bar girl. 'We need somewhere to stay.'

She laughed. 'Course we speak English. You're in Denmark.'

Although we had five days in Scandinavia's second most populated country (after Sweden), we'd spend two of those in Copenhagen with friends and one on the road. So we needed to find Viggo and Anja quickly, then get out to explore.

'There are many beautiful hotels in Aarhus,' said the girl in the bar. 'So, so beautiful. You would love them.'

RG and I held hands and shared a smile.

'You are rich right?' the girl went on. 'They are very expensive. We're an expensive city and an expensive country.'

We ended up staying for one night in a rundown hostel for around the amount we paid for Gianni's hideaway in Siena, almost exactly a month earlier. That blowing our budget, I picked us up a cheap dinner from a nearby supermarket.

When you say Denmark, Norway, Sweden, Finland or Iceland to somebody, there's a good chance they'll think force. Thor and his thunder. Magnús Ver Magnússon and his explosive power. The Vikings and their constant conquering. Brigitte Nielsen. Whether or not they like their image, Scandinavians have come to stand for conflict over the centuries.

But according to norden.org, an online hub for everything Nordic, town twinning – that great bastion of cultural tolerance and acceptance – actually started life here *before* the second world war. Which meant, if that was true, there were attempts at bringing European towns closer together before the town twinning RG and I had been exploring over the last couple of months had become official.

Going by the website, it all started with Thisted in Denmark and Uddevalla in Sweden. The roots of the relationship lay in the formation of the Nordic Association in 1919. It was designed to strengthen relationships in the Nordic group. It wasn't until twenty years later, in 1939, that Thisted and Uddevalla 'twinned'. Seventy-five years on, it appeared they were still going strong. There remained tensions between Denmark and Sweden though, highlighted not long before our visit by Kristina Axén Olin. Then mayor of Stockholm, Kristina thought it would be a good idea to support a local campaign by wearing a promotional t-shirt. It had bravely declared:

Stockholm – capital of Scandinavia

The morning after arriving in your twin, we hit the streets.

'Aarhus – Danish for progress,' promised the city's guide and map. Which was a lie, because we looked it up and that was *'fremskridt'*. If Aarhus was going to tell porkies about what its name meant, it should really have said it was 'beautiful people'. Because they were everywhere. Wandering, cycling, sitting. In every shop, on every street corner.

After two months on the road, RG and I were managing to pull off the opposite of the Aarhus look. But fashion didn't matter any more (to me). We had less than a month to go, and just 12 more twins left to visit.

We didn't spot any signs of the Swansea-Aarhus connection in town. No red telephone boxes like in Waldbronn, no *Platz* like in Eppingen. Aarhus appeared to be a big, sleepy, harbour town, full of handsome folk and not much else.

'What shall we do?' I asked RG, after yet another bread-and-ham lunch.

She flicked through our guide book. 'Old Town and botanical gardens, please.'

With RG and I getting on better after Berlin, my mind returned to the twinning movement. A plaque and *Platz* were fine, but they were just markers of moments, a cake and candles – a sign that at some point the twinning really mattered, perhaps one day, or maybe over one weekend. *But what about long-term relationships?* I thought. *They, surely, are what Europe needs for a happy, healthy, peaceful and prosperous future.*

The further we travelled, the more people who got in touch about our adventure, the more mayors and twinning secretaries we met, the more friends and family back home we spoke to, the clearer it became that town twinning – so new and exciting back in the 1950s and 1960s – was losing its place in the modern world. The more truth we uncovered, the less I wanted to face facts. It was becoming obvious that town twinning had been usurped by social media and social networking.

But it seemed – hearing the leaders of France, Germany and the UK in the news debating who should be in Europe, and seeing independence parties across the Continent growing in strength and popularity – all this new technology was doing a poor job of creating meaningful relationships.

'If the heart falls out of town twinning,' I said to RG, as we descended the steps into the Viking museum, 'then, well, town twinning just becomes something empty, clinical and commercial – like Facebook.' I sighed.

If you like history, visit Aarhus for its Viking museum. Refurbished in 2008, the Vikingemuseet was so much more than a mere collection of artefects. Heading underground we stepped into the exact spot where the Vikings had founded your twin town close to 1200 years before. With its model city from around 980AD, animation of the Viking attack on the area, and displays that depicted moments from Aarhus's history, the museum was a hidden treat.

As the evening drew in and our concentration levels started to wane, we picked KT up from a university car park a little out of town and hit the road. Our wallets were bare and, after a quick stop-off to see friends in Copenhagen, we were heading to another of Europe's most expensive countries.

Rob

Hi Rob,

I've adopted Newcastle as my home town (or toon as they
say in these parts). It has some interesting twins including
Bergen in Norway and Malmö in Sweden.

I know a bit about Bergen, like there's a festive tradition
that one of the City's Christmas trees comes from there
and the Mayor is part of the lighting celebrations. I can't
find anything about Malmö though. I'd love to know
what goes on there.

Good luck with your trip and making connections.
I look forward to hearing from you.

Michelle

34 · Malmö
Twinned with Newcastle

—

In which there is a gratuitous nudity

Dear Michelle

There was a deafening roar. Thunderous. Then a cacophony of thuds, screeches and screams, repeating every couple of seconds, but ten times worse every few minutes. As I looked up, I just hoped they weren't coming for me.

We'd arrived in your twin town the day before, crossing the same bridge I'd soon be sitting beneath. It was the second remarkable structure we'd crossed that morning. The first, the Storebæltsbroen or Great Belt Fixed Link, had taken us from Korsør to Nyborg, two coastal Danish towns.

But it was the Öresund that had stolen the breath from my lungs. As we'd emerged from the tunnel on the Danish side and climbed the long ascent of the bridge, there was no spotting the end of it. The thing went on and on and on for almost eight kilometres. That's five miles of bridge.

'I have to go and see the bridge, up close and personal,' I said to RG, as we were crossing from water back to land in KT.

'Now?' she asked.

'No. But before we leave,' I replied. 'I'll just pop over and take a look tomorrow. On foot. Bet it'll be a lovely twin town walk. Wanna come?'

'Not sure I fancy it really.'

'No problem,' I said.

The day after driving it, I said goodbye to RG in Kungsparken and set off on my morning stroll. Looking at my phone map, the bridge looked a healthy amble from the park. I'd need to go through the old town, then cross the neighbour-hoods Fridem, Bellevue, Gamla Limhamn and others, before emerging under the crossing.

'You've got suncream on?' I heard RG shout, just about in earshot.

'Probably,' I shouted back.

A heavy rain shower had greeted us as we'd arrived in Malmö on the Monday. In proper tourist fashion, we'd found an Irish pub and nipped in to watch the football. Today was completely different. Thirty degrees and a single solid sheet of blue overhead.

There's nothing quite the same as getting to know a city on foot. Like the lines, scars and blemishes of our skin, I like to think a city's terrain reveals the true personality of the place. It was only on foot, for example, that I started to see Malmö as a multicultural blender, as a patchwork of the old, the new, the green, the shiny and metallic, and as a playground where beautiful people liked to get their bits out.

Around 170 different nationalities were living in your twin at the time of our visit. From the Arab quarter where we were staying to the districts where Bosnians, Yugoslavians and Polish dominated, Malmö was defining a new identity: hanging its industrial overalls in the locker and donning the colours, sounds and sights of a modern city.

A grass bank guided me a lot of the way around the coast. I passed several piers licking out into the Öresund Strait before spotting something hazy and curv-ing on the horizon. The faint outline of the bridge appeared, flicking right like a reptilian tail.

I walked on, my t-shirt sleeves riding high thanks to the straps of my backpack, until I reached the marina at pier 10. The plan was to rest my legs after an hour's walking and tuck into my Subway roll. Then I spotted a naked man on his back taking in the early summer sun, his arms and legs in star shape. All of a sudden, the six-incher in my backpack became less appealing. I carried on.

The nudists at the Ribersborg beach weren't like any nudists I'd seen before – and I'd seen quite a few. During family holidays on the Isle of Wight, we'd sometimes stumble upon nudist beaches before scarpering when my parents had noticed their mistake. But usually that was escaping from fiercely tattooed, overweight, pale-skinned Brits, their flesh pinking like salmon. Malmö nudists were, like their clothed Danish foes, a beautiful breed.

I found a spot a little further around the coast to eat. Looking out to a distant and hazy Denmark, I tucked in. Then my star-shaped friend came to sit next to me.

He said something in Swedish.

'Sorry. English?' I said, mid-bite, staring straight ahead.

'Yes, yes, of course,' he replied. 'You're in Sweden. We all speak English here.'

The naked man continued to chat to me as I ate my food. He asked why I was in Malmö so I told him about our trip. While looking straight ahead. To the water. Never to the side. Never to him.

'Because of the line of latitude,' he said. 'Newcastle and Malmö are on the same latitude. That's what I heard.'

It's rare to have a conversation with someone you don't look at once. But then it's rare to have a conversation on a bench with a Swedish man who has his tackle out. Just halfway through my food, I wrapped it up, stuffed it back in my bag, said goodbye and plodded on.

'Good luck,' shouted the naked Swede, pendulating in the slight sea breeze. 'Enjoy the best bits of our city.'

In 2011, Swedish and Danish television came together to produce the crime drama 'The Bridge'. The first series started with a body on the Öresund bridge. It appeared to have been severed in two, with one half laying in Swedish territory and the other in Danish. After investigation, it turned out the body was made of two separate corpses.

I sat on the Swedish side, below the point where the bridge took flight from Malmö, and looked up. There was a deafening roar. Thunderous. Then a cacophony of thuds, screeches and screams, repeating every couple of seconds, but ten times worse every few minutes. Despite this chorus of cars and trains, I shot my arms up in celebration. I'd made it in just over a couple of hours. From where I was sitting, the bridge now looked like the jaw of a giant crocodile, with its series of struts snapping towards me like teeth.

Over the din of the transport I heard a text arrive from RG, whose plan was to spend the day relaxing and absorbing culture in some local museums.

'I have some bad news. It's to do with Malmö. Tell you later x'

We spent the evening coming third in a pub quiz and trying to soothe my vicious sunburn. Before RG could share her news with me, we got chatting to two Americans behind the bar. They'd moved to Malmö for work a few years earlier. Although a bit of a quiet place, the tall and bulky Ade told us, there wasn't a big enough reason to move away from the city.

The sun had set and temperature had dropped as we left the city centre pub and headed for the motel. Malmö had started to sleep. In another park, we swung on swings and caught up.

'You would've loved the exhibition,' said RG. 'The history of rock music in photographs. Thought of you while I was going around.'

I pushed the swing RG was sitting on. 'But what's the bad news?' I asked.

'Oh yeah, that.'

Rob

PART III

THE FINAL PUSH

Rob

Hey, brilliant!

That means that you will have to come to Cheltenham
too! :-) It's twinned with Goettingen.

You can get in touch with the Cheltenham German
Club here: www.cheltenhamgermanclub.webs.com

Betti

35 · Goettingen
Twinned with Cheltenham

—

In which Rob gets frustrated

Dear Betti

In Lower Saxony on Tuesday 26th June 2012, in the early evening, having just read the bright blue booklet that celebrated the 30th twinning anniversary of Cheltenham Spa and Goettingen back in 1981, it all made sense. Why town twinning had started and was still just about going. Why my girlfriend and I were having so many ups and downs. And why this adventure had had to happen and now.

The whole town twinning thing, I realised, was built on humans and human emotion. It challenged us all – helped us question who we really were. It was about our identity and our destiny. But at its most fundamental, it was about the warmth of our flesh.

Hurricane Festival, on the other hand, had made our flesh cold. The rain had come into Scheesel on the Sunday afternoon and sent us towards your twin via a cheap motel. Six months before our trip I'd bought tickets for that festival. Six months we'd been waiting to see our favourite bands. Sadly it wasn't to be.

'The best way to see Goettingen is to take the tour,' said RG, looking at a leaflet she'd picked up in the tourist office.

'Cool. Who does the tour?' I asked.

'Me,' she said.

Despite our drenching at Hurricane, we were both in a good mood. After the Big Fallout on the road to Eppingen, then Sweeping Under the Carpet in Berlin, it seemed we'd hit the perfect note and weren't drawing another breath. Either that or we'd lost the energy to bicker.

RG took the lead in your twin town. We started in the *Altas Rathaus*, just off the main market. Now more showpiece than anything else, the old town hall building started life in 1270. Around the late 1300s, it became the city hall. Work has taken place through the centuries, with the gothic porch and hallway added in 1884. We gawped at the artwork and spoke to the wrinkled lady inside the building about town twinning. She pointed us towards the *Neues Rathaus*.

With my time management worse than ever – missing the cathedral in Worms the final straw – I listened to RG when she suggested taking her tour before hitting the new town hall. 'Just follow,' she said, putting her arm around me. 'Just follow me and listen.'

So, without any question, I did.

'This,' said RG, not far from the *Rathaus*, 'is the most kissed girl in the world.' She was pointing at a bronze statue of a girl carrying a fat goose in her right hand and holding a sunflower in her left. 'Recently graduated students give her a peck on the cheek when they leave uni.'

'Great story,' I said. 'I wonder—'

RG took me by the arm. 'No time for questions on this tour I'm afraid, sir,' she said. 'There's so much to see in Goettingen.'

Physicists, shoemakers' guild-houses, churches, 15th-century half-timbered homes, more churches, one of Germany's largest libraries with over 5.9 million books and bits inside, the theatre, yet more churches. And that was just the first 19 stops on the 40-stop tour.

'We're not going to have time to do it all,' I said to RG, trying to hold her back. 'It's gone lunchtime already. Didn't you want ice cream?'

'Sure you don't want to hear about number 20?' she asked.

Ten minutes later, we were standing by the plaque of Cheltenham Park.

'It was named after Goettingen's English twin town in 1976,' said RG, flailing her arms around like a tour guide. 'Inside, you'll find a reconstruction of Rohns bathing house, which, I think you'll find, was the first public bathing house in the town, built in 1820. There's also a swan pond.'

'Remarkable. Brilliant. But what was that bad news back in Malmö? You still haven't told me,' I said to RG, thinking back to her earlier text. 'Don't tell me we've found another couple of twins that aren't really twins?'

RG stopped walking. 'Malmö and Newcastle? Pretty sure they're twins. No, I was probably just texting about the ice cream I couldn't find. Anyway, don't interrupt your tour.'

At the entrance to Cheltenham Park, RG decided to wander back to town while I headed towards the new town hall. She was determined to find a launderette so we could remove our festival stench. I was determined to hear the story of a twinning that I was about to learn dated back to 1951.

The *Neues Rathaus* couldn't have been more different to the *Altas Rathaus*. At first glance, it looked a bit like a hospital. But, as I stepped inside, it *really* looked like a hospital. Lots of glass, lots of stone, lots of smartly dressed people stuck behind desks.

'Ah. You will need to speak to Herr Meyer, Mr Meyer, Wolfgang Meyer,' said the lady tucked around the corner from the entrance. 'He is our *Oberbürgermeister*. He is very happy on the town twinning, as you say.'

I beamed. 'Brilliant. *Danke*. Where is Mr Meyer?'

'I am sorry. He is not here today. You will need to come back in two days.'

'Oh for god— But I won't be around in two days,' I said through my teeth.

'I am sorry. We celebrated 60 years of *Partnerschaft* last year. You know?'

I picked my head up off the floor. 'I didn't know. Oh. Great.'

'Yes. Our *Oberbürgermeister* would tell you all about it. But he is not here.'

Just as I was about to ask if the German language had the phrase 'rubbing salt in a very painful wound', the receptionist handed me two little books. Both, it appeared, marked anniversaries of Goettingen's twinning with Cheltenham. The fatter one was from 2011, to celebrate those 60 years the receptionist had mentioned. The thinner, brighter blue booklet had been designed 30 years earlier. I was holding a relic.

Sitting in the waiting area of the town hall, I thumbed through the older piece of literature before moving on to the one from 2011.

The people in the bright blue 1981 booklet were younger than those in the later one. Not just because the people from the 1980s had aged in the latter but because, it seemed, the youth of both towns were once more interested in the relationship. With hair bobbed, permed or dangling, with rims thick and shorts too short, the boys and girls on pages 12 and 13 of the 1981 booklet looked ready for the twinning adventure that awaited. In the 2011 version, which was still packed with brilliant stories, everyone looked a little more pensionable.

'The concept of town twinning will always remain as new and fresh as those people throughout the world who devote their energies to the task; and this is the idea which will inspire the citizens of Cheltenham and Goettingen as they face the future years of partnership.'

I read this final paragraph of the older booklet to RG over Pot Noodle dinner.

'And that's its biggest challenge,' I said, slurping a loose noodle into my mouth and dribbling a little sauce down my chin. 'The Bernhards and Elkes and Normas and Christianes and Maries – they're amazing people, but they're not new and fresh any more. What happens when that generation disappears? When the people who created town twinning because of that nasty stuff that happened in the first half of the last century die? What happens then?'

RG wiped the sauce from my face. 'One of two things, I reckon. It either goes behind more closed doors, like in Poitiers and Porto, and disappears for good...'

'Or?' I asked.

RG stopped chewing. 'Or you do something about it.'

We spent the last hour in your twin town taking photos of frogs in the walled garden, and collecting our washing from the *Waschsalon*. Sadly, we ran out of time to get in touch with the German society you mentioned. But there's always 'in two days'.

Rob

Ello Rob.

So I'm from Winchester, which is all sorts of lovely if
you've not been. Pop down when you get a chance.

Anyway, I've no idea why, but Winchester is some kind
of triplet town. It's twinned with Giessen in Germany
and a couple of others.

Go forth and get invading/researching.

Cheers,
George

36 · Giessen
Twinned with Winchester

—

In which dinosaurs take over

Dear George

'Why do we only go to the official buildings?' RG asked me as KT crawled into a multistorey car park. 'I mean it's great we're speaking to people. But surely it's the individuals who make town twinning what it is. Isn't it?'

'Yes. But no associations have got back to us. And it's almost impossible to track them down,' I replied, ruffled. 'Remember the man in Château-Gontier we couldn't find? At least when we go into the town halls we meet *someone*.'

RG sighed. 'But they never know anything.'

'Well you don't even come into them any more,' I snapped.

RG got out of the car faster than usual. 'Fine. Nice. Thanks.'

'I'm sorry. I... I didn't mean it like that. I'm tired.'

We hugged it out and headed through the busy shopping centre, across a footbridge, past a 20-foot long crocodile, and down some steps towards a dinosaur. Giessen, twinned with your hometown, awaited.

'Look at me, look at me,' bellowed RG, running up to the head of a T-Rex and climbing inside. 'This place should be twinned with Jurassic Park.'

Iguanodon, Coelophysis, Dorudon, Purgatorius, Smilodon – you name it, we spotted it. Though we couldn't actually name anything until we had the handy *'Urzeit in Giessen Entdecken' Stadtplan*, our guide to prehistoric Giessen. And even then, we couldn't pronounce any of the words.

We'd picked up the booklet from an information centre off the main square. As I'd walked inside, the young German twosome had given me the biggest, broadest, warmest smile. A boy and a girl. But then I spoke, asking if they knew English. The lad, in fully buttoned check shirt, turned to the girl.

They muttered something about *Entdecken* and *Dinosauriern* and kept saying, 'How do you say?'.

Outside in the sticky sunshine, I found RG sitting on a wall near a mammoth.

'What did you discover, dinosaur hunter?' she asked.

'That they're *Dinosauriern*,' I said.

'We knew that.'

'Yeah.'

There's only so much wandering lost around small German towns one can do. Only so many cobbled streets and Megaloceroses one can take in. Though Giessen did feel a little different. For a town of around 76,000 people, where 24,000 of those were students, it seemed a little subdued.

'You destroyed most of us here,' a middle-aged lady in the *Rathaus* told me. 'It was the year 1944. You fell the bombs and we suffered.' I'd popped in to ask about your twin.

'I know nothing of the town twinning,' she went on, clenching her fists. 'That is for the Astrid but she is not here. We were destroyed in the war. You destroyed.'

RG had headed off to the botanical gardens while I'd started to dig deeper into the bombing. It seemed odd to me that a small town in the middle of Germany would be such a target for the Allies. What, I wondered, did Winchester's twin have hidden up its sleeve?

All I knew of Winchester before our visit to your twin was it had a cathedral. I thank the New Vaudeville Band for that info. Until today, I'd always thought their 1966 hit single had told me everything I'd ever need to know. For example, if I were to take my gal to Winchester, the cathedral would do nothing to stop her leaving. Not even rings its bell.

The cathedral, of course, still stands, over 1500 years after it started life as a humble Anglo-Saxon church. Many of Giessen's ancient buildings didn't have such an easy life, sadly. If you speak to the rotund lady in the *Rathaus* like I did – she may well have just been walking through the building snapping at English visitors – the Allies destroyed over 75% of the town.

But why Giessen?

Alone in the *Rathaus*, hearing rumours of a town twinning oracle who went by the cosmic-sounding name Astrid, I wandered up and down a staircase. I saw nothing. But then a hand touched my shoulder.

'The town twin man?' asked a short man in a floral shirt.

Before we could do formal introductions, he was whispering something about not really being allowed to do this. His pass took us through one set of doors, then another. I got excited.

'We are finding for Astrid,' he said, looking around like we were robbing the place. 'She is your answer.'

'But she's away today, no?' I asked the stranger.

His phone rang. He made a lot of noises of agreement. He nodded.

'I must go,' he said, touching a colleague on the shoulder as he tried to pass.

They spoke in German. They mentioned *'Partnerstadt'*.

'Hello,' said the new, taller, thinner, more wrinkled man. 'Follow. If you will be kind.'

A minute later, we were creeping around the level above. Furtively again, my new partner in crime swiped us through a door. 'Come this way,' he said, looking over my shoulder. 'I will lead you to a special person.'

'Astrid?' I asked.

'You know Astrid?'

This went on for another ten minutes. With every new guide came fresh promises of the elusive Astrid. By the time I'd slinked back outside into blinding sunshine reflecting off the concrete that seemed to make up large chunks of your twin town, I was looking to the heavens for this lady. But she never appeared.

During my aimless wanderings around the town hall, one of my many guides had answered a question on the bombing. Why Giessen? Why would the Allies pick on this seemingly inconspicuous little central German town?

Opened in July 1925, Flughafen Giessen was the town's first airfield. It was built on a site where airships and aircraft had been landing since 1911. By 1929, the site had a station building and hangars. And by 1938, it was lit by a beacon and bolstered by yet more hangars. Giessen, the seemingly inconspicuous little central German town, was armed and ready for war.

In 1945, American forces took control of Flughafen Giessen and turned it into a depot for the US army. Rumour has it that Sgt Elvis Presley, who was living in nearby Bad Nauheim, visited the depot. According to my guide, there was an ID photo in a local museum to prove it.

'No wonder they tried to flatten the place,' I said to RG, who I'd found in the middle of a daydream inside the botanical gardens. 'They had loads of munitions here, and planes.'

'It's so peaceful now,' said RG, smiling.

Apart from a group of chubby Spanish tourists, we were the only visitors to Giessen's *Botanischer Garten* that afternoon. We lost ourselves – and each other – along its winding paths. As a distant bird serenaded us, a thousand bombs fell in my mind.

With just a fortnight of our three-month adventure remaining, we were heading towards the place where it had all begun. We were heading back towards war.

Rob

Hello Rob

You may find it interesting to know that I live in a twinned town. High Wycombe is twinned with a town in Germany called Kelkheim, which is near Frankfurt. Both towns have an economy initially built around furniture, I think.

Let me know what you find.

Gareth

37 · Kelkheim
Twinned with High Wycombe

—

In which a big man makes an irresistible offer

Dear Gareth

Imagine for a moment it's summer 2012 and you've spent the last two and a half months on the road. You've been on the Continent in pursuit of a newfound passion. The past ten weeks have made you rugged and handsome and full of grit and vigour. Your girlfriend has been there throughout, supporting you.

You pull into a little town. It's suspiciously quiet, like something out of a Spaghetti Western. A couple of people wander by, eyeing you strangely, sizing up your mule (you've come into town on a mule). You're intrigued by this place so you swing by the local tourist office. Straightaway you're glad you did.

Kelkheim was a town twinning geek's dream.

I walked up the steps to the tourist centre like I was John Wayne and it was a saloon. I ignored the lady asking me to stop and walked on until I reached Beate, a smartly dressed woman with wavy blonde hair and a half-smile.

'*Guten tag,*' she said to me.

'*Guten tag,*' I replied, now fluent in international introductions. '*Sprechen sie Englisch?*'

'Yes,' she replied.

I'd left RG downstairs, fending off questions from the lady I'd walked past.

'Good because I'm from England and I'm looking for information about the *Partnerstadt* relationship of your town and High Wycombe. My name is Rob. I'm new in town. What can you give me?'

Beate marched over to me and stood a couple of inches from my face. 'Rob. Today we are very busy. I will try to help with our historian. Take a look around.'

Beate marched off into another room.

The tourist centre was a shrine to Kelkheim's twinning relationships with High Wycombe and Saint-Fons in France. There were trinkets, paperweights, badges, a bell, a beer mug and something that looked oddly like a bondage paddle but might have been a decorative wooden spoon. The latter was a present from High Wycombe back in 1985, the year the agreement was signed.

As RG joined me upstairs and started to take photos of the mementos, Beate marched back in. 'John is coming,' she said, again an inch from my face.

'John?' asked RG.

'Who are you?' said Beate, now so close to RG's face I could see my girlfriend's eyelashes wobbling with Beate's breaths.

'This is my girlfriend,' I said.

'John Provan,' said Beate, the words marching from her mouth. 'He is a historian of the town of Kelkheim. He is American. He will come and speak to you and go to the town with you and answer your questions.'

Our eyes lit up. 'Really?' I said. 'That's brilliant. We—'

'I wish I could help more. But we have an event at the weekend and there is a storm and we do not know how to do it.'

'It sounds stressful,' said RG.

Beate half-smiled again.

Twenty minutes later, a giant American man called John was weaving us through the streets of Kelkheim in his Audi estate. This man, we discovered, was a war aficionado with a Zeppelin obsession. Born to a German mother and American father in Ohio, he'd relocated to Kelkheim in 1977 and was now the local historian.

'Excuse me, but the whole area is rich in history of the war, my friend,' said John, concentrating fully on the road and never turning. 'Hm, the street is closed. Excuse me, but we'll need to go another route.'

One of the first things they teach you when you're growing up is to never get in cars with strangers. Twice I'd done it now. The other time, years earlier, I'd pulled up in a car park in the middle of Dartmoor, seen the raised eyebrows on a man in the car next to me, and jumped in. The man was a Torbay Investigator of the Paranormal. We were going letterboxing as part of my moonwalking adventures.

In John's Audi estate, I asked him a question about town twinning. He responded with a war fact. Thinking back, every time I asked John a question about town twinning, he replied with something about the war.

'I have a few collections, I do,' said John, as he pointed out some former furniture makers' shops. 'When people scrap things, I go salvage. Some people would call my home a museum.'

Recordings of Third Reich war criminals at the Nuremberg trials, confidential photos of JFK having lunch at US barracks in nearby Hanau, the last interview Sgt Elvis Presley gave before leaving Germany. John had it all, recovering most of it from closing barracks, like the one in Giessen.

'I find this stuff interesting, I do,' he told us.

After a tour of a local hotel – closed for refurbishment and yet another treasure trove to our guide – John drove us to his favourite lunching spot. Perched half-way down a steep hill, it would offer views north towards the Taunus mountains, he promised.

'Hey, hey,' said John, pushing open the stiff door. 'Hey, anyone here?'

We made our way out to the rear balcony, where the Taunus opened up to us like Lake Lucerne all those weeks earlier. RG gave me the warmest smile. But the pub, sadly, was closed.

'Maybe it's something to do with the football. Germany versus Italy. Big game,' I said.

John shrugged. 'Excuse me, I'm not really the soccer kind of guy.'

On our way back to the tourist centre, we popped into the local museum, where John told us he gave talks on war history and – we learnt as he got chatting to a short Englishman with a long, thick, wiry beard – wood.

'Wood? Like furniture?' asked RG.

'Yes,' said the bushy-faced man. 'Look around. Kelkheim is famous for its furniture making. No, *was* famous for it. Like High Wycombe in England.'

'Your twin town,' I said.

'Yes, our twin town. You know High Wycombe? You're *from* High Wycombe?' he asked.

We explained our journey. Ten countries so far, 37 twin towns visited out of 45, just the two of us, three months. 'All to get to the bottom of town twinning and tell the folks back home what goes on in their twin.'

'Well you can tell them we're as into wood and furniture as they are,' said John, pointing to a beautiful cabinet.

Back in the 19th century, High Wycombe was the place to go for chairs, the Windsor being its most famous product. But your hometown's love affair with the chair goes back to the early 17th century, when woodworkers started making good use of the abundant Beechwood from Buckinghamshire woods.

Kelkheim's relationship with furniture-making was a little more forced, our whiskered friend explained. When farming failed to pay the bills, those who lived around the Taunus mountains turned to weaving linen. When the mechanical loom put pay to that as a career, locals went down the mines. But there wasn't enough limonite for everyone. So, by the mid-19th century, a couple of Kelkheim families tried making furniture.

An industry began. Wood from the mountains became chests of drawers, beds and cabinets for the people of nearby cities, like Frankfurt.

'Look at these pieces,' said John, beaming. 'Look at the craftsmanship. People devoted their lives to their craft. But today, what do we have?'

It doesn't take a historian to see the plight in industries like furniture-making. Standing between two specialists, both brimming with practical knowledge and an understanding of craft I knew I'd never reach, I thought about the internet again. Perhaps without the web, we'd put more value on stuff, I wondered. We'd understand that quality is a result of time – that fast facts, quick production and instant messaging aren't necessarily the answer. After all, it wasn't helping town twinning.

As we stepped outside, Beate's storm began. Puddles appeared like springs around our feet as we said goodbye to John.

'Stay in touch, yes?' he said, as we ran back towards KT. 'Email me. Though I never check my email. Goodbye.'

Rob

Hello,

I am an artist/illustrator from Margate in Kent. Margate
is twinned with Idar-Oberstein in Germany. Margate has
a very tacky kitsch degenerated reputation but in recent
years has undergone quite a transformation especially in
the arts and with its new gallery the Turner Contemporary.

I produce work based on Margate and try to give it a positive
reputation, especially with the locals. I have never visited its
twin town but have always been curious about it.

I think maybe your journey could be a great start to
a community project, bringing the locals together,
encouraging youngsters to expand their horizons
and learn about different cultures.

I look forward to hearing from you and wish you
a successful journey!

Lucy

38 · Idar-Oberstein
Twinned with Margate

—

In which our adventurers make a discovery

Dear Lucy

I need to admit something. I only know Margate because of 'Only Fools and Horses'. 'The Jolly Boys' Outing' episode. I know it's by the sea, there are fairground rides, and chips come by the bucket. That was back in the late 1980s though. Today, I guess it looks similar to then – but with fewer visitors. Idar-Oberstein, on the other hand, looked like nothing I'd seen before. A place I would never have believed existed if you hadn't sent me there. What a treat of a destination it would be for the community project you mention.

We arrived the night of the Germany versus Italy match. Spirits in the town were high. After a little negotiating with a fierce old lady in a hotel just around the corner from the main high street, we had somewhere to stay. And five minutes later, we found ourselves strolling towards the town centre.

'Why is every shop selling gems?' asked RG.

'Idar-Oberstein – City of Gems.' I smiled.

RG was right. Every second shop was in the gem trade. Stalls outside presented an array of stones – reds, browns, purples and blues. As we climbed the gentle hill towards the centre of town, it was difficult to move for agate and jasper.

The warm sun had begun to set and the tourist centre was closing for the day. Just before the shutters came down, a smartly dressed young German lad told us to come back tomorrow.

But the next morning, Idar-Oberstein had a different feel.

'Why's it so flat?' I asked RG, smiling at the few locals slumped outside the cafés.

RG stopped. 'Um. You know what we missed last night?'

We'd forgotten the football. Mario Balotelli had scored two goals to knock Germany out of the cup. And now everything just felt a bit sad. But it didn't last. In the town square, a woman was singing what sounded like Portuguese songs, while old men clapped and children sprinted round in circles.

We spoke to the same lad in the tourist centre. He introduced us to some new favourite words like *Felsenkirche*, *Edelsteinminen*, Schloss Oberstein and *Spiessbraten*. They were a church in the rocks, gemstone mines, a castle overlooking the town and a speciality Brazilian meat dish – features of a town of around 30,000 people, couched between Frankfurt and Luxembourg in the far south-west of Germany.

'All in Idar?' I asked.

'Idar-Oberstein, yes. Once we were Idar and Oberstein. But today we are one.'

We started a steep walk towards the *Felsenkirche*.

'Why have we never heard of this magical place before?' I asked RG, as we climbed the fierce hill to the church. 'It's some sort of wonderland.'

'Because it's a tiny town in Germany with a massively interesting history that sadly *no-one's* ever heard of,' she replied. 'God bless town twinning.'

To get to the church (*Kirche*) in the rocks (*Felsen*), we walked along a cold, damp, echoing tunnel. At the other end, the world's happiest man greeted us, as soon as he could drag himself away from his newspaper.

'You're the English,' he boomed, shaking the church a little. 'Oh, how I love the English. I like everything of the English. I am a mad supporter of Liverpool Football Club.'

With that, he started to sing 'You'll never walk alone', the team's signature tune, at the top of his voice. To aid international relations, I joined in.

The *Felsenkirche*, our new friend told us between eruptions of the Gerry & The Pacemakers classic, dated back to 1482. And like the owls of Uelzen, it came with its own myth.

Two brothers, Wyrich and Emich, once lived in Burg Bosselstein, the castle above the church. Both men fell in love with beautiful Bertha but knew nothing of the other's feelings. While Wyrich, the older of the two, was away, Emich took full advantage and got off with Bertha. They soon married. Wyrich, as you can imagine, was gutted. And furious. In a moment of vitriol, he lifted his little brother and hurled him out of the castle and over the rocky cliffs to his death. Moments later, Bertha died from a broken heart.

The surviving brother instantly regretted what he'd just done and sought advice from the local abbot, who suggested building a church in the exact place his brother had died. Seeking forgiveness, he did it. In fact, he put so much of his energy into creating the *Felsenkiche* that he died on its steps the day it was to be consecrated. But not before God had granted him absolution, in the form of a spring inside the church. Wandering around, we followed the sounds of dripping water to Wyrich's spring.

We stepped onto the balcony, where Idar-Oberstein opened up before us.

'Enjoy tonight,' shouted the man at the desk as we left. 'You're lucky to be here for the celebrations.'

'*Danke*,' we replied, stepping back into a damp tunnel to leave.

RG turned to me. 'What celebrations?'

'No idea,' I said, my voice echoing around me.

RG and I had started dating not long before our town twinning adventure. During an early dinner date, she'd told me about her samba obsession. She was part of a band, she said. She played samba. As always happens to me during those first shared moments with someone, I didn't listen to the details. In this instance, I'd replaced '*tamborim*' with 'sequined dress' and 'drumming' with 'sexy dancing'.

'That's samba,' she said, as we returned to the heart of your little German twin town. 'Look.' Her face lit up.

As we sat for dinner on a warm balcony overlooking the square, a handful of decorated women did their thing below. As a drummer beat out an African rhythm, Idar-Oberstein's populace tapped their feet. But not RG. As soon as we'd polished off our churrasco-inspired *Spiessbraten*, she was up on stage, showing the Germans how to do it. It turned out that my earlier mishearing and imagining wasn't far from the truth.

Any other time, I'd have smiled at my love's nifty footwork. But this evening I felt an odd pang of embarrassment that I couldn't shake. As her bottom bumped into the other dancers, I looked away. I could sense her looking over for my support. My heart sank. After a few days of breezing along, knocking German twins aside like jungle vines, my emotions had tripped me up again.

I picked up a flyer from my table and read it from my lap. All of a sudden so much made sense: the gems, the samba, the Brazilian barbeques. But, sadly, not the hollow feeling in the pit of my stomach.

Rob

Rob

Please investigate Bonn, twinned with Belfast.
Then come to Belfast.

Gillian

39 · Bonn
Twinned with Belfast

—

In which things go from bad to worse

Dear Gillian

'I can't wait to meet Sabine,' said RG, swiping through her phone, grinning.

'Sabine?' I asked, parking on a kerb outside a small house in a town called Bad Godesberg, which wasn't too far from your twin town.

'Yes, Rob. The lady who lives *there*,' said RG, pointing at the house. 'We're staying with her tonight. I booked yesterday.'

'Really? Who is she?' I asked.

We'd spent the morning in a mine just outside Idar-Oberstein, the twin before yours. It'd confirmed what I'd learnt at the samba event. The little German town's love of all things Brazilian had come from its gems.

Our guide around the mines had explained – mostly in German but with a few words in English – how agate and jasper miners had taken their skills to South America in the 18th century, when local German supplies of these semi-precious stones had run dry. They returned with some beautiful knowledge: mainly how to marinate meat in onions and seasoning and create *Spiessbraten*, my new favourite dish.

'She's super lovely,' said RG, skipping back to the car from Sabine's to help me take our bag over. 'We're in her children's room.'

'And her children don't mind?' I asked.

'Guess they're away.'

'And her husband?' I asked.

RG shrugged. 'I don't know, Rob. Maybe she doesn't have a husband. Maybe she's a lesbian. I have no idea. Why can't you just wait and see?'

Sabine was a short, chubby-cheeked, middle-aged English teacher with big red lips and a thing for young men. She now rented out her children's old bedroom to guests through airbnb, a new online holiday rental phenomenon. While RG got dressed for dinner in our bedroom, Sabine told me about her evening's date.

'A barrister, eh?' I said, keeping my distance.

'Yes, a *barista*,' said Sabine. 'Very talented with his hands.'

I laughed awkwardly. 'Um, great. Thanks for sharing.'

RG and I would walk the one-and-a-half hours into Bonn the next morning, we decided. This evening we'd pop to a local restaurant in Bad Godesberg, then watch the final of the European Championships. Sabine had suggested a pub on the Rhine. It sounded perfect – a few beers, the football, the river, a gentle sunset. The sort of evening to pump new energy into a couple of weary travellers. Sadly, it didn't go to plan.

With just ten days left of our quest, RG exploded in a shower of daggers. Not one bit of my character escaped the attack. Beer-fuelled, she held nothing in. Frustratingly, she was right about most of it.

'You've got a massive chip on your shoulder,' I slurred in retaliation, which was like fending off a Rottweiler with a carrot.

'I've got a massive chip on *my* shoulder?' she shouted. 'Well, look at *your* shoulder. *There's* a chip. Like a massive one. Bigger than mine.'

'Leave my chips out of this. You're acting like a child,' I said.

Sabine's breakfast the next morning was delicious. If a little silent.

'Bonn then?' I asked RG, sinking a fresh mint tea.

'Yes.'

'Great.'

'Good,' said RG. 'And her date's a *barista*, not a barrister.'

'Fine. Whatever,' I said, like a grumpy teen.

The 90 minutes into Bonn were as painful as the 90 minutes Italy had endured the night before in the football final. We spoke about five words to each other on the walk along the river. None fun, none complimentary. All completely functional.

Lunch? Yep. Drink? Ok. Thanks.

During that walk, my mind was 99% sure of what needed to happen. I needed to not be in a relationship with someone who could be so cruel about my chips. We both knew it. One more wrong word or action and that'd be it, whether we'd completed our circuit of twins or not.

'I visited Bonn on a school trip,' said RG, breaking the silence at the city gates.

'Really? You didn't say you've been here before.'

'I think I did.'

'I'm terribly sorry. I must not have heard.'

'That's ok. Sometimes I don't hear things either.'

'That is true.'

We'd gone from great team to good team to poor team to weirdly polite team. Each eggshell beneath our feet was now more delicate than the one before. We were analysing every word like it could be our last.

'Shall we visit the Beethoven House?' asked RG. 'I went with school.'

'I think that is a good idea.'

There were no hints at Bonn's twinning with Belfast on the streets. No signs, no plaques, no Belfaststrasses that we could spot. There were just parks, outdoor markets, and a striking, guano-splattered bronze statue of one of the most famous classical composers of all time.

Standing outside Beethoven House, RG remembered we needed to sneak down its side to find the way in. We did so without alerting any of the million tourists who were clawing at the front door.

I didn't realise until near the end of the tour that Beethoven House was actually Beethoven's *house*. This was where he'd lived from 1770 to 1772. Inside we saw Joseph Karl Stieler's famous portrait of the composer penning a masterpiece, his grey hair curling wildly above his head. Then the final grand piano to ever feel the flesh of Ludwig's fantastic fingers. Before a collection of the great man's ear trumpets, which he used when his hearing had started to fail aged just 30. In Digital Beethoven House next door, about half the tourists from outside were tapping at computers. RG and I sat at two spares and wrote special

Beethoven-branded emails back to our loved ones. Afterwards, RG told me she'd written to her sister. I could only imagine it was a cry for help.

There was something very Belfast in the Bonn air. Perhaps the students ambling around, the friends playing football on the field, the sense of culture at every corner. Nobody in the *Rathaus* could tell us why the two were twinned, but it just felt right. Like it was meant to be. Belfast and Bonn, I liked to think, shared a bloodline. They were both cultural catalysts, a capital and, controversially, former capital, and they both sat on important rivers. They were cut from the same cloth.

'I'm sorry,' I said to RG before sleep. 'For sparking you last night.'

She smiled. 'Look, we've got just over a week till we go home. We're 40 or so towns in. We're nearly there. We just need to put up with each other for a little bit longer. Then we can work out what to do.'

'Do you want to break up?' I asked.

'I just want to enjoy the rest of this adventure with you. Let's get to the end. Together. Ok?'

As we kissed good night, the light flicked on outside our room.

'What if she tries to seduce me?' I whispered to RG.

'I'll wish her luck,' she replied, with a smile in her voice. 'My love...'

'Yes?' I asked.

'When can we have ice cream for dinner?'

Rob

* * *

Not long after returning from the trip, I had this saddening Twitter exchange with Belfast City Council:

Belfast City Council @belfastcc
@robselfpierson hi Rob, we're not actually twinned with Bonn or any other European cities – sorry!

Rob Self-Pierson @robselfpierson
@belfastcc Ooh, really? Everywhere online suggests you are. Were you once twinned? (There seemed such a shared spirit.)

Belfast City Council @belfastcc
@robselfpierson nope sorry, not that we're aware!

Hi,

My hometown Fareham (ugly, postwar) is twinned with
Vannes in Brittany (v pretty, complete set of medieval
walls, loads of timber framed buildings, location of my
first ever experience of eating prawns with the shells
on - a life-changing moment if ever there was one)
and Pulheim (no idea, probably in Germany).

Try Pulheim – I need to hear a story that might match
my Vannes one.

Good luck!

Robin

40 · Pulheim
Twinned with Fareham
—

In which RG regrets finally getting her own way

Dear Robin

They were lovely. Just completely over the top and camper than Lionel Blair riding a pink unicorn. Which made where they lived feel even weirder.

'Are you sure this is right?' I asked RG, parking outside what looked like a printers in an industrial estate.

We compared the address in our booking confirmation to the road name and number in front of us. They were the same.

'Maybe they'll do some business cards for your new business ventures,' I said, loosely holding my girlfriend's hand.

Upstairs, the two young men – both handsome, slicked, manicured and dressed perfectly in trousers and shirts – were making costumes for Gay Pride. I walked in on them mid-tape and asked them for their wifi password.

'Yeah, Robert, it's in your room. On a little card.'

'No, no, Alessio, it's not. Don't you remember? You moved the card to another room.'

'Ummmmm, Mario, listen to me, my dear. It's there. I put it there with my own beautiful hands.'

'Alessio, don't go talking to me like that. Not with guests. Sorry, Robert.'

'Don't talk to Robert when you're talking to me.'

This went on.

Back in the room, RG had found the wifi password. 'It was on this.' She held up a little card. 'Are they arguing?'

The couple's tiff didn't seem to have affected them an hour later, as we said goodbye and headed into Pulheim. Mine and RG's had though. Our kisses were cold and our hand-squeezes limp. It appeared my girlfriend had just one thing on her mind.

'I really don't think you want ice cream for dinner, my dear,' I said.

Pulheim was made up of twelve smaller places, including four former independent municipalities and eight boroughs. They came together on the first day of 1975, becoming a city six years later. Pulheim was originally one of the four municipalities. At the time of our visit, it was the principle town of the city of Pulheim.

I learnt all this inside the new city hall. I'd popped in for a nose around and to see if I could find a good spot for ice cream lunch. It was the usual story. I spoke to a very pleasant woman at reception who told me there was only one person who knew about the Pulheim-Fareham connection, but she was away. She'd be back tomorrow, when we'd be visiting our final German twin.

'If you had just one day in Pulheim, what would you do?' I asked.

'One day is long enough,' replied the lady, with a cheeky smile. 'The Stommeln windmill. Visit the Stommeln windmill.'

'And where is that?' I asked.

'In Stommeln. And the Brauweiler Abbey.'

'In Brauweiler?' I guessed. She nodded.

By now, all of our small German twin towns had started to merge into one. Apart from Neustadt an der Weinstrasse and Idar-Oberstein, none really stood out. Each was either green or grey, medieval or ultra modern, surrounded by huge, dense forest or autobahns. The people were friendly, but never wasted a breath on unnecessary politeness or chat.

'I don't think I can finish this,' said RG, letting a slop of ice cream fall from her spoon back into its sundae glass. 'Don't ever let me have ice cream for lunch again. Please.'

'But...' I smiled. 'Deal. No more ice cream lunches. Ice cream dinners?'

On the queasy walk back to KT, we spotted Farehamstrasse. But still the twin-related road signs, town signs and plaques felt like markers of something historical, of yesteryear. Not of blossoming cultural ties. They were installed years and generations ago to celebrate the hope that comes at the beginning of relationships. Today, they were more extinguished candles, many blown out decades earlier.

This was never meant to happen. Placing your twin's name on the sign that would welcome people to your town was a statement. It was bold. It gave equal footing to the two places – it said, *We stand together as one, us and our twin, sharing everything that is good about ourselves.*

How long, I wondered, looking over to the street sign, *before Farehamstrasse loses all meaning to those who live on it?*

Twenty minutes later, we'd found Brauweiler and parked up.

Brauweiler Abbey, we soon learnt, was infamous. It was in this Benedictine monastery that the Gestapo did innumerable and unthinkable things to anyone who didn't fit the Nazi template. The social and political 'undesirables'. They would be imprisoned, tortured and sometimes murdered in this 11th-century place of God.

'It's beautiful,' said RG. 'Look at the doors and windows.'

Its beauty – its terracotta-and-cream facades, cockerel-topped steeple, cobbled walkways and geometrically perfect hedges – made its past seem all the more horrific. There was no English translation of the boards that appeared to detail exactly what had taken place in and around the abbey. That was probably a good thing.

After leaving the abbey, we spent the next half hour driving around Pulheim's many parts in sombre and reflective mood looking for its windmill. Path after track after lane – KT's sump taking more of a battering with every wrong guess – there was no sign of it.

'I'll just pull over here and we can agree our story about seeing the mill,' I said to RG, picking another random road.

'Ok,' she said. 'It was big. Really big. With sails. White sails.'

'Agreed. And a dragon,' I added. 'Made of chocolate. And—'

RG stopped me. 'Why don't you just pull up next to this windmill?'

The Stommeln windmill – which we'd somehow managed to sneak up on and park underneath – was the symbol of Stommeln, a former municipality like Pulheim and Brauweiler. In contrast to Farehamstrasse (a symbol of town twinning), it appeared unapologetically wherever Stommeln needed representation.

'I wonder how these towns do it,' I pondered. 'How can you bring together this cluster of individual places under one name and keep them all happy? Do that back home and there'd be riots.'

'Shared identity,' said RG. 'Maybe that's why town twinning isn't doing well.'

We stood outside the car and peered up at the picturebook windmill.

'How do you mean?' I asked.

'Well, it's like you have to give and take. Maybe you've got to share a little culture to get a little culture. And we're not great at doing that back home, like those ladies back in France were saying to you.'

'Back home in England?' I asked.

'Yeah,' said RG. 'That's what people have been telling us. Over here they're better at it. And we've seen how easy it is to just cross borders and hop into other countries. And how everyone hugs and kisses. More sharing, right?'

It made sense. I mean how would the people of North Boarhunt, Titchfield, Southwick and Wickham feel if they became Farehamites? And how would you and your Fareham friends react if you had to become West-Portsmouthites? And how would all these people deal with having to embrace one another?

'You'll need to have opinions on all this sort of stuff, Rob,' said RG, as we crossed the Rhine and headed for Witten, our final German twin. 'Not sure you can be the offical twinning expert otherwise.'

Rob

Rob

Witten in Germany. I know nothing. Shed some light.

Darcy

41 · Witten
Twinned with Barking
—

In which KT comes to the rescue

Dear Darcy

'You realise we're in North Rhine-Westphalia?' said RG, as we pulled up behind a petrol station for lunch.

I'd come full circle. Around a year earlier, I was drinking beer and eating bratwurst outside a caravan in Hoerstel with a group of German youths who couldn't speak English. I could almost smell the North Rhine-Westphalian air and taste the raw North Rhine-Westphalian pork.

'Yup,' I said to RG. 'The North Rhine. My second home.'

I was reminded how green and luscious North Rhine-Westphalia is when we wandered around an enormous lake behind the service station. A quick stroll near 'that nice bit of water' turned into the sort of hike Lewis and Clark might've undertaken when mapping America.

'I can imagine just disappearing after this trip,' I said to RG, putting the leftovers of our lunch back into KT after our walk.

'Really? I can't wait to get home.'

I dumped our tote bag back in the boot. As I let go of its strap, a great slop of creamy rollmop landed on RG's hoodie.

'Why did you do that?' she asked.

'I didn't mean to,' I said, staring at the mess.

'Why did you just drop it in? Why didn't you let me do it?'

'I can put a bag in the boot myself, thanks,' I said, clenching my jaw.

'Well you can't, can you?' she replied. 'But you can drop fish over my stuff.'

'Maybe I *will* disappear after this trip actually,' I said, playing my ace card.

'Good idea,' said RG, cleaning her hoodie.

I slammed the boot, dropped into the car and put my foot down to take us to Witten and finish the trip as quickly as I could. But in a moment of red mist, I forgot where we were. As I pulled onto the left and curved right around a blind bend, an old VW estate clunked around the corner towards us.

In many respects, a BMW Z4 was completely the wrong vehicle to take on a three-month road trip. With her compact boot, leaking hood, lack of spare tyre, addiction to petrol and just two seats, KT was totally ill-suited to 10,000 miles through every sort of weather and terrain Europe had thrown at us. But the split-second she gracefully dog-legged around the oncoming VW made her the ideal travelling companion.

The next morning, we carried out our usual routine: showered, brushed our teeth, packed our big black bag and fit it snugly into KT's boot, and prepared to speak to an efficiently friendly German lady in the tourist information centre of Witten.

'*Guten tag, sprechen sie Englisch?*' I asked like a robot.

'Yes, hallo. Can I help you?'

RG explained our adventure. She said we were in Witten because our friend had suggested we visit her twin town. We wanted to know about the history of the twinning and learn about Witten.

We flicked through the pile of leaflets the tall, thin, blonde lady gave us.

'We started to exchange people in 1948,' she told us, her charming approach to words making me smile. 'But in 1979, we were officially partnership. It starts with the Kingsley Hall church community.'

I looked up from '*Stadtmitte Übersicht*' which was all in German and therefore wasted on me.

'You know a lot about the twinning with Barking,' I said with a grin.

'I can read it from here,' she replied.

Our twinning expert was actually a Googling expert.

'It's great that you have come here from Barking to visit us. I will tell everyone I meet when I go to the home. Although the home I have is not in Witten. I would not like to live here.'

'You're not from Witten?' I asked. 'We're not from Barking either. Our friend Darcy is.'

'I am from a town near here. It is into the forest. If you are here today, you must go to the forest. It is beautiful.'

We said goodbye and crossed the town square as the sky began to drip on us once again. Within minutes, we were drenched – both of us in our shorts.

RG spotted something.

'You seen that?' she called to me through the thudding raindrops.

Was it a public toilet? Was it an ultra-cool museum exhibition? Was it a piece of temporary fencing? We couldn't tell. But it was emblazoned with numerous place names from around the world, including Barking and Dagenham.

'These must be all Witten's twin towns,' said RG, taking my photo by the sign.

'They have a twin in Nicaragua?'

'Must have,' she said. 'Maybe it's so councillors can go on tropical jollies.'

'Yeah. Stupid town twinning,' I joked. 'Just a bloody waste of money. Stupid excuse to send councillors to wherever Nicaragua is, and turn public toilets into art installations.'

Before our wet walk in the Witten wilderness, we grabbed something called a *Fleischwurst* from a café that looked a bit like an O2 store mixed with an ice cream hut. Having enjoyed those barbequed North Rhine-Westphalian wursts in Hoerstel, I assured RG that it would taste a million times better than it looked. Sadly it didn't. It tasted a billion times worse.

'It's like lukewarm sick,' said RG.

'I know,' I said, dropping and spitting every last piece of *Fleisch* into the nearest bin. 'I want some of that cold meat spaghetti thing to get rid of the taste. And ice cream.'

Back inside the steamy warmth of KT, RG played us some tunes on her musical potato. She'd become quite the virtuoso since Cordoba.

'Perhaps that's the new career angle?' I questioned.

'Maybe,' she said, before launching into another rendition of something.

In her eagerness to show off the town she worked in but wouldn't want to live in, the lady from the tourist office had torn a map of the Hohenstein Naherhol-ungsgebiet out of the magazine. Hohenstein, we guessed, was a town close to Witten. Naherholungsgebiet? We had no idea.

It soon revealed itself as the forest the lady had recommended for a stroll. So with an hour free before our three-hour drive out of Germany and across the Netherlands into Delft, where things between me and RG would go from awkward to disastrous, we had a look around.

From the top of a sandstone tower, we watched the remainder of the day's storm flood over the German countryside. We saw the surface of the Ruhr, a tributary of the Rhine, turn speckled as yet another downpour coated the horizon.

'Starting to feel a little like home?' I asked RG.

Her eyebrows lifted and eyes widened. 'Certainly is.'

Rob

Rob – Deep Joy!

I've just discovered that my town, Kingston upon Thames, is twinned with Delft in Holland. I went there once on a school trip. It was lovely. I even bought my Mum a ceramic dish, she still has it – or so she assures me.

It's also, of course, the setting for 'Girl with a Pearl Earring'. So well worth a visit.

Enjoy, Andrew

42 · Delft
Twinned with Kingston upon Thames
—
In which there is a mysterious omission

Dear Andrew

Change of pace. Change of scenery. Change of feelings. As we wiggled between road works and under Dutch Spaghetti Junctions, life felt a little lighter. *Maybe it was Germany,* I wondered as we parked outside our hotel in the Delft suburbs. *Maybe that German seriousness had crept between me and my lady and taken the fun out of our relationship.*

We set off from our hotel just north-east of the city with a spring in our steps. Where the gravel path intersected the canal path, two beautiful cyclists ding-dinged their bells and smiled. I breathed in deep, trying to absorb some wonderful health.

'Look at the little houses on the canals,' I said to RG with a silly grin on my face. 'They look like big, fixed canal boats.'

'And look,' said RG, 'little houses for bikes, too.'

At this moment, as we held hands and bounced along the canal, not even the heavy sky, humid air and murky waterways could dampen our spirits.

'Wicked,' I said, tapping the bike hut. 'Lovely.'

Two hundred canal photos later, we reached another watery junction. Wafts of pungent fish floated before our noses and drew us left, between a million more cyclists, each more upright that the one before. We came to an open-sided caravan selling deep-fried something-fish. We watched as locals popped up to the counter in unspoken turn, like bees to a flower. After seeing five or six, we picked up the courage to give it a go.

'English people?' asked the man serving. 'What do you like?'

'You speak English. Great,' I said.

'You're in the Netherlands. Of course we do.'

'Funny,' said RG. 'They said the same thing in Denmark.'

We chatted with Martin as we devoured our fish, which apparently had more salt content per bite than if you were to eat pure salt sprinkled with salt. With stiff mouths, we thanked him for his suggestions to check out the Delftware factory, markets and, of course, canals.

'And what do you know about twin towns?' I asked.

'Nothing,' said Martin, and with that he was serving herring to another bee. 'Try the city hall. It's by the canal.'

An hour later, I'd walked a good few miles up and down the four billion or so canals of Delft. I'd cut up cyclists, barged children and seen Martin in his caravan five or six times. RG, wisely, had decided to pop into the city centre instead to see what she could find there. I ended up asking Martin for directions again.

Three minutes later, I was in a queue inside city hall, standing a couple of hundred feet from where I'd started. I could almost see the fish van through the window.

'Twins?' shouted the tall, dark-haired, flagpole of a man behind reception. 'Yes. Follow me.'

We burst through city hall like bank robbers, rushing out into the courtyard.

'There,' said the tall man, pointing at the lamppost towering even higher above me. 'Our *partnersteden*, or "twin towns" to you.'

I peered up. 'Wow. Look, Freiberg and Esteli and Kfar Saba and... where's Kingston upon Thames?'

My friend looked back up to the sign and smiled. 'Our *partnersteden*. We are proud to build these relations with you.'

'But I'm not there,' I said.

'That's great,' he replied. 'Now I am busy and have to run, like you say.'

He shook my hand and cantered back into the building.

I checked the lamppost again. Freiberg, I could see, had twinned with Delft in 1986 from 771km away. Esteli, in somewhere called NCA, had twinned in 1984 and was 9250km in the opposite direction to Freiberg. Kfar Saba in Israel had twinned with Delft back in 1972, when European twinning was still going strong. But nothing about Kingston.

Delft's market square was bigger than I'd expected. Instead of spotting RG looking through records or buying a cake from a little old lady, there were just enormous buildings, tall, ornate and gilded. The town hall looked like a beautiful earthy volcano shooting up from the square, while the Protestant *Nieuwe Kerk* (new church) fired skywards like a rocket ship.

With no sign of my other half, I stood for five minutes and listened to a local school's brass band fill the fishy air with trumpet and trombone. Then inside a local Delftware shop, I asked about the history of the Netherlands' answer to Chinese porcelain.

Back in the 16th century, factories had begun to pop up across the Netherlands manufacturing Majolica. This was a type of pottery finished with an opaque glaze. A century later, the Dutch East India company started to import porcelain from China. It was a big hit, especially the blue-and-white designs. As with anything popular, people started to copy it. Soon, the Majolica factories were producing their own blue-and-white porcelain or 'Delftware' for short. I expect that's what you bought your lucky mum.

'What a great story,' I said to the lady who was now on the phone. I handed her a plate I'd decided to buy for *my* parents.

As I went to pay, I remembered RG had my wallet. I patted down my legs to find my phone to call her. But she had that, too. All I could find was a musical potato in my pocket.

I stepped back into the square, the sun beginning to melt my skin. I found a fiver inside my coat. Severely dehydrated, hungry, lost and alone, I headed for the local currency exchange to see what I could get for it.

'You can get six euros for five pounds,' said the bespectacled lady behind the desk. 'Minus commission.'

'Great. Fine. Six euros should get me dinner,' I said.

'Minus commission,' repeated the lady.

'Which is how much?' I asked.

She tapped away into a calculator. 'Around four euros.'

'Four?' I questioned.

'Four,' she said, lowering her glasses. 'If I were you, I'd tell me no and hold onto my five pounds sterling.'

I swallowed the sweat-stained air and did as she suggested.

It took another hour to find RG. Another 60 minutes of dragging my salty, sweaty body around the canal paths of your twin. I saw pretty corner café after pretty corner café. I watched pretty people fly by on pretty bicycles. I started halluci-nating Matt and Sam bringing me a pint and congratulating me on 'doing that twin town adventure thing and becoming a proper European' but they had the heads of the Eldwedritsche from the Palatinate Forest. There may have even been two gay Italian guys riding a pink unicorn as well. Perhaps it was like a scene from 'Girl with a Pearl Earring'?

There's no telling how much of that hour was real and how much was dehydration-inspired. My only concrete memory is of a kindly old Belgian lady from Ghent, our next twin. She'd asked why I looked so strange.

'My girlfriend is gone,' I explained, a little in French, a little in English, a little in German and the rest in unicorn. 'Gone. Disappeared. And I'm here alone, without a home or money. This is my new life. I am now Rob from Delft.'

'*There* you are,' said a caramel-skinned human-shaped RG creature, sitting down beside me. 'Guess what. I've got your wallet, silly.'

I coughed a response.

'I know. I laughed too when I was drinking my coffee and chatting to the lovely guy in the café. Delft's super lovely. Innit?'

That evening, we spoke to my brother on Skype. He was all packed up and ready for a move back to England from Basel, where we'd visited him six weeks earlier. His second baby had arrived in the day and his cheeks were glowing.

'You'll get to meet her soon, bro,' he told me.

'Wicked,' I replied. 'You look happy. Red in the cheeks.'

He smiled. 'Might be the celebratory beer.' He pointed his camera towards his TV screen. 'Have you two seen this?'

As the image focused, I spotted the corner of my flat back home.

'It's the Olympic torch,' said my brother. 'It went through Waltham Abbey today.'

'Waltham Abbey...' I started.

'Twinned with Hoerstel, North Rhine-Westphalia, Germany,' finished RG, giving me one of her sweetest smiles of the trip.

Rob

Rob

So I'm from Nottingham, which has seven twin towns
(it's a tart of a city, let's be honest) of which five are in
Europe. Ningbo in China is clearly made up. Ghent is
probably the most charming.

Nottingham is known as the gun crime capital of the
UK, so it could be that twin cities have been chosen for
their link to violent crime. So beware. I do hope this
has been of some help, but if it's been of hindrance,
I apologise, but well, that may be useful too.

Martin

43 · Ghent
Twinned with Nottingham
—

In which three months of bickering bubbles over

Dear Martin

'Dodgiest hotel of them all,' said RG, walking in my shadows.

'It's ok,' I said, clutching my phone and wallet in my pockets. 'It's fine. We're fine. Nothing's going to happen out here in this weird, dark, spooky industrial park in Belgium. Everything's fine.'

It was late at night and we were in Ghent, twin town number 43 of 45. Correction: we were miles *outside* Ghent. As far outside Ghent as we could be while still being in Ghent. Our F1 hotel stood alone beside a disused railway line on the outskirts of the city. (I had a sneaking suspicion we were still closer to Delft than to your twin.)

Next morning, we donned our walking shoes, stocked up on supplies, bade our new F1 family farewell and crossed to the bus stop. After half an hour of staring at a dead road, we guessed buses didn't risk venturing this far out of town any more. We had no choice but to go on foot.

'You ok?' I shouted back to RG, after we'd walked about a mile down the featureless, rain-spotted street .

She continued to stare at the pavement and plod, her hood up, her hands deep in her pockets.

'You all right back there?' I tried again.

Nothing.

'Lady...'

'What?' Her eyes were glistening.

'You ok?' I asked.

Instead of slowing to check on my girlfriend, I carried on ahead. I couldn't deal
with it. The humid rain was drizzling into my face, my legs were heavy and my
once clear and excited mind was addled.

We reached an overpass that looked like a bridge we'd crossed in Paris in April.
Back then we'd had the naivety of the early town twinning organisers. We were
young, keen, spirited and hopeful. When the spring winds had bitten in the city
of love, RG and I had just squeezed each other harder. Back then, silence had
meant romance.

'The castle then?' I asked my travelling companion outside the tourist information office.

'Yes, let's do that,' she replied.

'Going to smile for me?'

Ghent was indeed as charming as you'd suggested it might be – even with the
occasional shoe hanging overhead from its phone lines. Near the ancient city
centre, tiny cafés and bars were hiding inside long brick buildings with stepped
faces. Awnings were the only giveaway they were there.

Inside the Castle of the Counts, RG and I tried friendly chatter with each other.
She snapped a photo of me staring out of the wee-stained window. I hid behind
some swords, hoping a quick burst of peek-a-boo might save our relationship.

But outside we had a proper chat. An adult one.

The outcome was my offer to drive RG to Brussels for her to get the train back to London. It'd be better for us both, I tried to explain. No more bickering, fighting, swearing, cursing, sulking. No more ups and downs.

'I'm finishing this,' she replied. 'We started it together, we'll finish it together. We can talk about our future when we get home.'

It was Wimbledon final Sunday. To give us time apart, I went to find a pub showing the Federer-Murray match, while RG explored your twin. Inside Patrick Foley's Irish bar, I met Michael, a young, fresh-faced lad from Leeds. He'd cycled to Ghent as part of a summer adventure. It was a family tradition, but this year, now he'd left college, he'd wanted to do it alone.

After a few pints, we were sharing everything. And by the time RG had arrived, he knew as much about her as I did.

'Good game of tennis, boys?' asked RG, shaking the rain from her hood.

'Oh, God, the game,' we both mumbled.

The evening descended pretty quickly after that. We dragged Michael to a Belgian restaurant, where we treated him to moules-frites and a few gallons of wine. We even gave the lucky chap a tour of the city.

'You've been here quite a while then?' he asked.

'A day,' we replied.

Arm in arm, Michael and I sang our way through the streets of your twin. We smiled and shouted 'hello' to locals and students, like an enlightened Ebenezeer Scrooge in stereo. We hopped bollards, sprinted down alleys and embraced like a married couple.

Michael wobbled home towards his campsite as we closed in on midnight. To this day, I don't know if he got there safely. RG and I, drunkenly starting the epic walk back to Uglyville, passed a live band playing inside one of the hidden bars. We veered in.

Most details from the rest of the night escape me. I remember asking the barman over and over again what time they closed and whether I could squeeze in one more beer. His answer was always that they'd close when the last person had left. I also remember pulling a man's dreadlocks.

'What the hell are you doing?' whispered RG, still a few drinks behind me. 'You idiot. You can't—'

As the chap turned to face me, RG looked away and stared at the wall.

'Hi.' I grinned then hiccoughed.

A few minutes later, I'd told Mr Dreadlocks most of my life story, from my time as a sick baby in Great Ormond Street to my moonwalking adventures around Britain and discovery of lots of town twinning signs. I remember him laughing a lot, but that was probably at my face noises.

At one point, I nudged RG. 'He'd like us to go back to his flat and smoke some...' – I started to whisper – 'naughty green cigarettes.' I winked.

And then I fell asleep. I later learnt I'd tried to spark a conversation between RG and most of the guys in the bar.

'And you kept asking them about town twinning and what their favourite twin town was,' said RG. 'And their favourite tennis player. And whether they knew Michael, because you loved him and thought he was great.'

We were halfway back to the hotel when the tears began to flow. First from RG, then from me. The alcohol had loosened our tongues and our hearts. As the heavens dumped all they could on us, we crumbled like a couple of early morning drunks. Which is exactly what we were.

The hurt, the accusations, the meanness, the spite, the jibes, the constant close proximity, the lack of freedom, the uncovering of the other's different tastes, the contradictions, the guilt trips, the anger. We disgorged everything. Even stuff that wasn't true. Brittany, Basel, Berlin, Prague, Delft – every argument, every insult, we covered them all and more.

We admitted that we missed our friends and our families. We shared that neither of us was strong enough for the other. Then we hugged and cried.

In three months, we'd slipped apart. With every new twin town, we'd learnt another reason for spending time in different places. Our common interests weren't enough any more. We were the worst example of twinning in Europe, and we had to do something about it.

RG drove us back into your twin the next morning – I was too dizzy, shaky and still overflowing with Belgian beer. We parked up and admired the city centre, with its markets, waffle shops and mustard sellers. Souvenirs stuffed safely in pockets, I stood in the central square while RG bought a waffle.

Before heading towards our penultimate twin, we stole some wifi from outside a café near the Irish pub.

'Oh dear,' I said to RG, whose face was covered in chocolate. 'I think recession's hitting international relations.'

'Why's that?' she asked.

'Nottingham's done a bad thing. It's just like Christiane in Poitiers warned. I think it's time to be officially quite worried.'

Rob

Hey Rob,

I was reading your website about the twinning of towns
and it made me think of my own home town, Wolverton
in Buckinghamshire.

It has only recently been twinned with a town in Belgium
called Ploegsteert and there's a really poignant story behind
it. Basically Albert French was a man from Wolverton who
fought in WW1 and died and was buried in Belgium.
This is where the connection comes from.

Can you tell me any more about the place and the man?

Take care,
Michelle

44 · Ploegsteert
Twinned with Wolverton
—

In which final tears are shed

Dear Michelle

Thank you. Thank you for leading us towards such a beautiful penultimate twin town story. For giving me and RG the excuse we needed to reconnect after such a tumultous three months. Thank you for 'Plugstreet', our Belgian barn adventure, Albert French and for the moment I broke down and blubbed like a baby.

Before we left Ghent, we'd already booked our final two nights on the adventure: the first was a room in a huge converted barn near your twin and the other was a room in a cottage in Montreuil-sur-Mer, the twin we'd almost forgotten. We couldn't wait to reach the French coast.

It was a short drive from Ghent to Ploegsteert. The roads were like those between our earliest twins, when we'd cruised around former battlefields in northern France. But now, in the middle of summer, the fields were in bloom.

We reached the barn in the early evening. The sun was doing its best to light and heat the tall, stubble-coarse grass that stretched in every direction to the horizon. Calling *'HELLO'*, *'BONJOUR'*, *'GUTEN TAG'* and the other greetings now in our armoury, we crunched across the gravel to the barn and knocked on the door. There was no response. So we crossed the courtyard and knocked on a kitchen window. Still nothing.

'Near enough all the funding gone,' I said to RG, while we waited in KT for our hosts to appear. 'Back in 2000, Nottingham City Council cut its budget. Completely. One of the articles said they're still funding small events with

Ghent and its other twins. But it seems that's just to show good will.'

'Pretty rubbish,' said RG, summarising my sentiments beautifully.

'Yeah. Goodbye town twinning?' My lungs filled and fell.

The barn owners appeared from nowhere half an hour later. They were a young family – slim, smiling mum, shy dad and teenage daughter. As a team, they cooked us a platter of meats, vegetables, salads and potatoes prepared in every way you can imagine. Stuffed, we headed to bed and slept soundly in absolute silence.

We woke to a cloudy warmth and a distant cockerel the next morning. It was Tuesday 10th July. In two days we'd be standing once again on a Channel ferry, waving to the White Cliffs. Laying below the barn's beams in the best bed we'd enjoyed in weeks, I pictured the moment we'd arrive again in England. The grinning teeth of Albion, the ferry groaning into port, every passenger taking the wrong staircase and getting lost among the lorries.

'What's up?' asked RG, fresh after a shower.

'I don't want to go home,' I said, squeezing my eyes shut and drifting back to disturbed sleep. 'I feel comfortable over here.'

Ploegsteert was a tiny way over the France-Belgium border, just under ten miles from Ypres. During the war, as the Allies took hold of Ypres to block the Nazis from French and Belgian ports, they nicknamed it 'Wipers' – a word they could all agree how to pronounce. Ploegsteert, a town we'd been calling 'Plerg-stare' since you'd asked us to visit, had a very similar story.

It was difficult to know where Ploegsteert started and ended. We began our hunt for its story at a crossroads. Beside a small stone war memorial, the humblest we'd stood and reflected by so far, we found the local archives. After a decent bit of French questioning, we learnt we should head to a small place called Comines. There, the short grey pensioner with curly hair and gold-rimmed glasses hanging around her neck had assured us, we'd learn a good story about Wolverton and Ploegsteert.

Like Bob Cratchett after the passing of Tiny Tim, my steps had slowed these past few days. I'd felt trapped between une rock und eine hard place. Here I was two days before the end of a three-month adventure wishing to be with a girl I loved but couldn't spend long periods of time with. Or without.

'Nearly done,' she'd say most days. 'We're nearly there. Nearly through it.'

When I'd returned from Hoerstel at the beginning of all this, filled with enthusiasm for a road trip around the Continent, this wasn't how I'd pictured it ending.

In Comines, we crossed a wide and quiet railway track. Long grasses suggested it hadn't seen a train for a generation or two. After three attempts at locating the international centre, we found a building that looked like a mix of greenhouse, hospital and airport. From experience, this was probably it.

'I think we're there, my dear,' said RG, walking in ahead of me.

I searched downstairs while RG went up. Pulling back curtains, I found nothing but more curtains. There were shelves filled with boxes and boxes stuffed with paperwork. But unlike in Waldbronn and Kelkheim, I spotted no certificates, cups or paddles.

Upstairs I discovered my girlfriend sitting with two young men, smiling.

'Where did you go?' she asked. 'Meet Jean-Christophe and his friend Matthieu. They're telling me the story of Albert French. It's amazing.'

'Ah, you are Mr Twin Town,' said Jean-Christophe. 'It is – my English is poor –

very good to be meeting you.'

I shook the tall man's hand.

'Please, sit.'

As I sat, Jean-Christophe shared the story of Albert French, the soldier whose tragic tale was the catalyst for the twinning between your hometown and Ploegsteert. Listening to every detail, I shrank in my chair and felt the blood in my extremities chill.

Back in 1913, Albert French was an ordinary Buckinghamshire lad. After a stint working in a chemists, he became an apprentice engineer at the local railway works. Then in 1914 came an exciting announcement: Britain was at war with Germany, and if you were over 18 years old you could join the army and fight for your country. But be quick – the war would be over by Christmas.

A year into the Great War, aged 16, Albert French joined the King's Royal Rifles at St. Pancras, Middlesex. He was tall and stubbled therefore nobody questioned his age.

Young Albert started his army life training in Chelmsford, Essex. Jean-Christophe showed us a letter the boy had written to his family. It revealed that his thoughts were focused on chocolate, having a good time, rising to the rank of lance corporal and getting a new handkerchief. Within seven months he would be dead.

'What happened to him?' asked RG, flicking through some paperwork Matthieu had printed for us. 'How did he die?'

'Allow me to read from his letter from the website mkheritage.com,' said Jean-Christophe, clearing his throat. 'It says: "*I am very sorry to have to write to you and inform you that your dear son was killed in action on June 15th. He died as every true soldier wishes to die – doing his duty nobly for King and*

Country. He was doing some sand-bagging on the parapet of the trench when four bullets from a machine gun hit him and he died instantaneously.'"

'He was building a protective wall and got torn to shreds by bullets?' I asked.

My English was too much for the two men to understand, but their raised eyebrows showed they understood the sentiment – and my disgust at such a waste of life.

'You now must visit the grave of Albert French from Wolverton,' said Matthieu, showing us its location on a map. 'And you return soon. We are to build a new memorial here: Le Centre d'Interpretation de Ploegsteert. Or "Plugstreet", yes? It is easier for you to say from England?'

The two men smiled at us. We shrugged, confused.

'How you and the Americans called our town. It was better to say for them.'

'Plugstreet?' asked RG. 'Sweet. Wolverton and Plugstreet, connected thanks to Albert French, the boy who shouldn't have even been here.'

Albert French had left England for France on May 2nd 1916. By May 28th, he was in the trenches at 'Plugstreet'. On Thursday 15th June – while back home in Buckinghamshire his sister May was writing him teasing letters, 'soon to be sweet 17 and never been kissed' – young Albert French was killed.

We approached the site of Albert French's burial place as many visitors from England had over the years. In fact, it was this pilgrimage that had sparked an idea: Wolverton and Comines/Ploegsteert should be twin towns. So, on 27th May 2006, almost exactly 90 years after this young lad from Wolverton entered the trenches in Belgium, the charter was signed, close to where his body now lies.

We stood on the road between the boy's gravestone and Ploegsteert's Memorial to the Missing, a great neoclassical open roundhouse, ghostly white and deathly silent. A small group of British schoolchildren scribbled furiously in notepads outside the memorial, each trying to capture their feelings in words and pictures.

Inside the cemetery, we found our gravestone. It said simply:

C/7259 RIFLEMAN
A. E. FRENCH
KING'S ROYAL RIFLE CORPS
15th JUNE 1916
AGE 16

As the school group's coach pulled away, I left RG in the cemetery and headed to the memorial. With each step, my breath quickened and fingers lost their heat. I felt like I was dragging my feet through mud and that the air around me had thinned. Then my eyes filled and I felt my face quiver. As I stepped inside the structure, whose walls were engraved with the names of 11,386 men who had no known grave, tears poured from my eyes, down my cheeks and stained the stone I stood on.

I saw RG approach and tried to compose myself but failed. I blubbed something about the waste of life and wailed something about loving her and tried to repeat my desire that town twinning *had* to continue. Too much depended on its future.

Rob

Hi Rob,

When we met briefly I said Slough was twinned with France and I was right!

Slough is twinned with Montreuil, France (Since 1988).

It was lovely to meet you and RG and I hope you enjoyed the rest of your birthday on Sunday. Paul looked at the pictures on Face Book. There is a nice one of you and RG and a good couple of us at the table as a group.

Good luck with your travels!

Best Wishes and Be Happy!!!

Natalie and Paul x

45 · Montreuil-sur-Mer
Twinned with Slough
—

In which Rob and RG say a fond farewell

Dear Natalie and Paul

For years I'd been somehow connected to the wonderful world of town twinning. From the moment Mr Finnan had interrupted my French class to invite me to Germany, to the time I'd enjoyed morning tea with hunched Norma in Waltham Abbey, town twinning had been my mysterious friend. It had intrigued me so much I'd just spent a quarter of a year trying to understand everything I could about it.

Now today, one day shy of exactly three months since leaving Dover for the Continent in my sports car KT with my girlfriend by my side, I was closing in on the end of the odyssey. This was it. Montreuil-sur-Mer. Twin town number 45, and probably the most misleadingly named yet.

'I love the sea,' I said to RG as we pulled up outside the cottage we'd booked for our final night. 'Think I was born to live *sur la mer.*'

'Yeah. Can't wait,' said RG. 'Not going to be very warm. But at least we can dip our toes in. It's gonna be so good.'

Inside the cottage, we met a tiny lady who could speak no English. Talking almost fluently in some form of French, RG and I established that our room was across the hallway, there were some lovely restaurants in town, we should see the ramparts because of their role for the British army in the war, and we weren't actually near the sea after all.

'Pres la mer, oui?' I'd asked.

'Non,' the lady had replied, before saying lots of other mystery things.

After lugging our big black bag into a guesthouse for the final time on the trip, I told my girlfriend I needed some air. The ramparts were calling. RG stayed behind and read her book.

Montreuil-sur-Mer was a pretty town, walkable in just over an hour. Strolling its cobbled streets in search of the ramparts, I learnt Victor Hugo had stopped here for a few hours in 1837. Like us, he'd felt shortchanged that it wasn't by the sea. But the town's characters and charm inspired him enough to write his most famous work, *Les Misérables*.

Across a few town squares, between a couple of ancient buildings leaning in so far from opposite sides of the street they seemed to want to kiss, and under an archway, I reached a track that led to *les remparts*. A little further along, I joined Promenade des Remparts, which led in a smooth curve, away from a citadel and, as far as I could tell, around the edge of the town. Walking along the walls, the wind picked up and pushed me into a trot.

I sat at a bench that faced towards distant trees and hills, and there I did very little except take deep breaths and try to sort out my life.

'Right, Rob,' I said to myself, out loud, 'this is it. You're here, at the end of your trip. You've been planning this for years and you've done it. That means you can celebrate. Well, once you've worked out what's next.'

A train chugged along the line at the bottom of the hill, away into the distance and out of sight. As it disappeared, I thought back to the moment I'd taken in the town sign on the outskirts of Waltham Abbey and seen so many other 'Twinned with...' messages around the country. I remembered the moment the glands in my neck had tingled in excitement at the thought of visiting Hoerstel, and that moment I realised my curiosity was going to take me much further than North Rhine-Westphalia.

A white-haired couple wandered behind the bench, followed by a hunched lady talking tunefully to the sparrows. To me they were Bernhard and Elke, Sunday strolling, and Norma, organising a little adventure for her feathered friends. The strengthening wind continued to blow cloaks of rainless cloud over the horizon like it had so often since we'd arrived in Douai back in April. I wrapped my coat around me and took out my phone.

'Come into town,' I messaged RG. 'Be lovely to share this time with you x.'

We met up back at the citadel and decided to pay a few euros to explore the grounds and learn a little history of your twin. The giant, protective ramparts I'd just walked dated back to 887AD, around the time France had become a kingdom and ceased to exist as West Francia, home of the tribal Franks. The name 'Montreuil' came from *Monasterium* – the town started life as a monastery, where relics from the East were brought and stored. The more I read from the signs and in the booklet, the more I fell for your twin.

'I know this is the last twin, lady,' I said to RG, as we stood at the top of the citadel's bunker, 'but let's take town twinning out of town halls and give it back to the people who make it work.'

'How do you mean?' she asked, taking a tentative step down into the darkness.

'I'm sure we've both been thinking it,' I went on, reaching the echoey bottom of the steps. 'Twinning. It's about towns and people. It's not about civic halls and inward investment. It's about people's stories, people's shared experience. It's about our desire to explore, our curiosity, our hunger to see and live in other cultures...'

We walked along the dank walls of the bunker.

'I've loved the pride of the people we've met. The happiness so clear on the faces of the people who've shown us their towns or told us their stories – John Provan, the guys in Frascati, the lady in Douai, Tim in Brittany, the bloke on the bridge in Prague, Ana's parents. None of those people *had* to help us with anything, but every one of them did. And they wanted nothing in return.'

RG pointed to a display board that told us these bunkers were built in 1845 to defend the town against the Prussians, then were used as Field Marshall Haig's HQ when the Allies were defending the Somme.

'I know we've had some tough times in the last three months,' I said, 'but we've laughed a lot. Not just at me pulling people by the dreadlocks, but with new friends. New *European* friends. And that's what this was all about, right?'

'Sure was,' said RG, letting me vent.

'Shut all this stuff behind doors and gates or lock it at the top of city halls and what's the point? In a way it doesn't need to be organised. Encouraged perhaps, but not labelled. We should all *want* to visit the small towns our fellow Europeans live in because they're great – the towns and the people who live in them.'

RG stopped me. 'There's no point telling *me*. I know, I get it. I've been here for every second of this thing. You need to encourage everyone else.'

That evening we ate moules-frites in a tiny café in the town centre. As we slurped down the sauce, we laughed at memories of our night in Ghent, when we'd dragged poor Michael around the city and treated him to his first taste of mussels. Looking back at what we'd achieved, we laughed and smiled a lot.

'I'm glad you came,' I said to RG. 'I know it's been pretty tough at times and we've both nearly killed each other often, but... it wouldn't have been the same without you. I really mean that.'

'I'm glad I came too,' she replied, putting her hand on mine. 'It wouldn't have been the same without me.'

We were still smiling the following morning when I showed RG the vista from the ramparts. We sat on the bench and looked out. The wind was still blustery but the view to the horizon was serene.

I turned to my girlfriend. 'Guess we should go and get our ferry,' I said, putting my arm around her. 'Time to head back to Blighty as a couple of proper Europeans. Shall we?'

RG turned to me and snuggled into my neck. 'Let us,' she said.

Rob

THE
FUTURE

A few days after returning to the UK, I was sitting in the Angel with Matt and Sam. A lot had changed in just three months. My brother now had a new baby. Matt had a new, squarer haircut. I'd become a better European. And RG and I had split up.

'That's a shame,' said Matt. 'Never nice to break up with someone.'

'KT and I are still going strong though.' I took a swig of beer. 'I like to think of it as untwinning, me and RG. The relationship began between two people with similar interests but who long-term just couldn't make it work.'

'So what happened exactly?' asked Sam.

I tried to give a snapshot of the trip, starting back in Douai, moving down through France to the Iberian peninsula, across the mountains and into Italy then Switzerland then Austria, eventually onto Germany via the Czech Republic, up to Scandinavia, back through Holland, Belgium, France and home. I tried to balance stories of friction and disagreement with tales of monumental beauty. I tried to paint a picture of everything that'd happened in just 90 days – the war history, the deflating tyre, the sunrise, the mountains, the dreadlocks, Michael and John and Christiane and Rachel and everyone and everything. And a smile appeared on my face.

'Sounds pretty cool,' said Sam. 'So you're a proper European now?'

'I'm a *better* European. Definitely need to get over to the Continent more. While we all still can.'

I shared stories of political unrest in France and not feeling wanted in Portugal. The borders might start closing down, I scaremongered. The right could rise again and Europe could return to dark days. I passed on warnings from the town twinning people and locals we'd spoken to about Britain being detached from Europe.

'Sounds a bit scary,' said Matt, missing his mouth with a peanut he'd just launched into the air. 'Fancy another pint? Could get you a European one.'

'Amstel?' said Sam.

That summer, RG played samba at the London Olympics and gave up her job. Soon after, she moved to Portland in Oregon. I started to spend more time exploring the Continent, made lots of Portuguese, Italian and French friends in London and had a go at developing an online hub for town twinning – something I'm still working on today. I was also asked to write a script about an Italian filmmaker who travelled Europe at the beginning of the 20th century. Rino Lupo, I soon learnt, left Italy to become a better person and better filmmaker. It was only when he returned home he understood the enormity of what he'd achieved.

Finally, at the end of last year, I had a chat with Carlos, a young man from the Council of European Municipalities and Regions (CEMR). We spoke for an hour about the current state of town twinning and our worries about its future. I shared a few stories from my adventure, which he very much enjoyed. He said nobody had ever visited so many twin towns for the fun of it before. So he asked me to do two things. The first was to write up my stories and send them to him. The second was to come up with an idea to help him save town twinning from extinction.

I said I'd see what I could do.

Where to start? Mum and Dad and Dave and Nick for listening to my many town twinning tales over and over and over again. And dealing with my promises to 'finish the book next week'. Every week. Matt and Sam for the distant support and beers. Norma, Elke and Bernhard for sowing the seed and everybody else we met along the way. Frankie for illustrating the inside and Karina the out. Grayling for some wonderful typesetting and brotherly chats. Becca for being the world's best printer. Xander for some extra belief. Globetrotters London and Dark Angels for listening with a critical ear. JC for bringing a little France to London and helping me edit my stories. Pedro for introducing me to Rino Lupo and encouraging me to carry on travelling. Lorna and Laura for time and wine in the gîte. Harry for his keen eye. Falmouth for the space to think. KT for lasting 10,000 miles and beyond. And last but most importantly RG, my unstoppable travelling companion, confidante and muse. We did it, lady.

Sitting below the bells with Fabrice, banging the keys that rang them...

Within five minutes, the top hat was on RG's head and
I was sipping a pint that tasted oddly like colon.

We stood and posed before sweeping panoramas.

...KT, purring, climbed steep gradients and revealed hundreds of miles of nature...

Everything all of a sudden felt very right with the world. Very right indeed.

'You know the buyer of owls?'

Arm in arm, Michael and I sang our way through the streets of your twin.

Placing your twin's name on the sign that would welcome people to your town was a statement. It was bold. It gave equal footing to the two places...